Maria Montessori

Also available from Bloomsbury

Early Childhood Studies: A Social Science Perspective, Ewan Ingleby
Maria Montessori, Marion O'Donnell
Philosophy of Education: An Introduction, Richard Bailey
Playing Outdoors in the Early Years, Ros Garrick

Maria Montessori
A critical introduction to key themes and debates

Marion O'Donnell

B L O O M S B U R Y

LONDON • NEW DELHI • NEW YORK • SYDNEY

Bloomsbury Academic

An imprint of Bloomsbury Publishing Plc

50 Bedford Square	175 Fifth Avenue
London	New York
WC1B 3DP	NY 10010
UK	USA

www.bloomsbury.com

First published 2013

British Library Cataloguing-in-Publication Data
A catalogue record for this book is available from the British Library.

ISBN: HB: 9781441134721
PB: 9781441172655
ePub: 9781441185389
PDF: 9781441186546

Library of Congress Cataloging-in-Publication Data
O'Donnell, Marion.Maria Montessori : a critical introduction to key themes and debates / Marion O'Donnell.
pages cm
Includes bibliographical references and index.
ISBN 978-1-4411-7265-5 (pbk.) – ISBN 978-1-4411-3472-1 (hardcover) –
ISBN 978-1-4411-8538-9 (ebook) – ISBN 978-1-4411-8654-6 (ebook)   1. Montessori, Maria, 1870-1952.   2. Montessori, Maria, 1870-1952–Criticism and interpretation.
3. Educators–Italy–Biography.   I. Title.
LB775.M8O36 2013
370.92–dc23
[B]
2012041401

Typeset by Newgen Imaging Systems Pvt Ltd, Chennai, India
Printed and bound in Great Britain

Contents

Introduction

More than a century ago Maria Montessori's approach to education was completely out of step with everything done in schools. This book describes how the Montessori method evolved through direct observations of 'free' children in a prepared environment. Montessori's success in 1907 with young children learning to write and read at 4 years was revolutionary.

Readers of this book should keep in mind that overshadowing all of Montessori's medical expertise as a clinical paediatrician was her interest in mental health. Her research focus before graduation was on nervous diseases when she worked in the psychiatric department of the University of Rome. She treated adult inmates, some of whom were mothers with children also living in the asylum. Soon, her focus turned to the causes of mental diseases in children. To Montessori it became clear that mental deficiency needed to be treated as a pedagogical problem rather than a medical problem.

Beginning with clinical observations, she conducted trials with special needs children in the asylum, and they succeeded in learning to care for their personal needs, caring for their environment and learning the 3Rs (writing, reading, arithmetic) using her special self-correcting materials. Some of these children were presented to sit an open examination and passed whereas children in schools failed the exam. With the success of her learners' learning, Montessori was keen to do trials with 'normal' children attending schools where so many failed to learn. to read and to write.

It was 1907 before Montessori had her opportunity to work with 'normal' children. This book explains what Montessori did with these children aged 3 years to 6 years. She had no theory but began with practice. She planned to observe children who were free to move about and choose what they would do. A few materials were available to them which she had used with the children in the asylum. There were two rules to follow. First, children were shown how to respect the materials. Second, they were not allowed to interrupt anyone using a piece of material. Montessori observed the children using didactic materials and activities she had designed to help them gain control of their own movements and meet with success. Success was a key to happiness, to a positive state of mental health.

Observation of children revealed their natural tendencies. They liked to choose what to do, repeat the experience and then put the material back on the shelf. All their tendencies became the principles of Montessori education. Children learned to care for their own needs and their environment, becoming independent of adults – a key aim of Montessori education. Observations revealed some children were excessively anxious, tired, worried or had hostile feelings towards others. This meant these children were not 'free' (in mind) to perform their chosen tasks. Children were to become masters of themselves, not masters of others. Montessori considered mastery of the environment along with positive relationships to be indications of good mental health.

The Montessori teacher, a 'directress', presented each piece of material to each child individually using a short three-period lesson. She then moved away to allow the child to make discoveries. This could be referred to as 'directed discovery', whereby the child was able to explore and make new discoveries for himself. The directress was to be a researcher and keep detailed notes of children's discoveries. Montessori demonstrated how to keep records of observations about progress in development. This was a very new role for teachers. Montessori urged teachers in 1907 to be researchers by using observation skills, taking notes, reflecting and taking action.

The teacher prepared the environment and was responsible for providing conditions for learning and an interpersonal climate. Included in the conditions was an anxiety free environment with no tests, no exams, no prizes, no punishments, no competition among students' standards, no time tables and no homework. Establishing a friendly interpersonal climate contributed to good mental health which had everything to do with each child's feelings towards his learning environment and his feelings about his own ability and self-esteem. Providing conditions conducive for each child to be successful led to happiness which Montessori believed to be a key to the life of the mind.

Mental health today

Behaviour in schools is said to be a reflection of society. Today there is an alarming increase in the mental and emotional needs of children. One in three children is reported to have some form of mental problem. Many children can be described as having an autism spectrum disorder displaying anxiety and depression from an early age. Behavioural issues are common with high percentages of students being banned or expelled from schools. Researchers in Australia have found that ADHD is the most common diagnosis of young children by paediatricians (Murdoch Children's Research Institute, May, 2012).

Perhaps it is time to look at Montessori education more closely to find answers to the mental health problems children experience today. Montessori's first Children's Houses contained a system of mental treatment which normalized the behaviour of children.

4 Maria Montessori

Dr Crichton Miller, a peer of Montessori wrote

> That doctors of medicine and professors of psychology were saying that her work would eventually make the nerve specialists superfluous and if the Montessori method was established in all schools, alms-houses would need to be established for psychologists.
>
> (Kramer, 1976: 264)

The Foundations of Montessori Education

1

Nurture and nature

Throughout history many philosophers and theorists put forward their views about the education of children and some suggested teaching methods. The idea that experiences in the early childhood years could have an effect on development and adult life was advanced by John Locke (1632–1704). He proposed that the newborn child's mind was 'like a blank slate' and that all experiences were important. He believed that social and environmental experiences would affect character and mental abilities in later life. Advice given to parents included encouraging a child's curiosity by answering questions with respect which in turn would lead to rational behaviour. Locke subscribed to *nurture* as being the force behind development because his view was that children could be shaped and influenced by their environment. Also he subscribed to a wide curriculum and each child should be dealt with individually. There are no reports of Locke putting his theories into practice (Boyd, 1921; Butts, 1955).

Half a century later Jean Jacques Rousseau (1712–1778) offered a view of childhood which changed the thought of many educators. His publication of *Émile* (1762), an imaginary child, excited readers about the importance and uniqueness of childhood. He averred that children were not valued and were often misunderstood. Some of Émile's experiences seem to be based on Rousseau's own childhood experiences described by de Beer (1972). To Rousseau, children were individuals who were capable of gaining knowledge as they explored the world themselves. He referred to stages of development, that children had different needs at different stages of development, suggested having sensory-motor exercises and giving children freedom. He was an advocate of *nature* viewing the child as a 'noble savage' who would develop intellectually if left uninhibited (Beatty, 1922: 76, 80). He tried to make a living as a tutor and teacher but was unsuccessful.

A century later, Maria Montessori (1870–1952) viewed childhood as a special period of life. The education associated with her name reflects her mindset as well as her lifelong research of child development, the learning process, the art of teaching and offering a wide curriculum. She incorporated both *nature* and *nurture,* but always overarching all else was her medical expertise as clinical paediatrician with an interest in mental health.

Maria Montessori was educated at home where she showed a keen interest in mathematics and then was enrolled in a technical school for boys to further her studies in mathematics and science. She developed an interest in medicine and became the first female Italian to study medicine when she enrolled to study medicine. Her first practical ventures in medicine focussed on nervous disorders, and by 1895 while still a student, she was working in the psychiatric department of the paediatric clinic at the University of Rome. It was there that she came in contact with children, institutionalized along with their parent-inmates. Montessori observed the behaviour of these children and interpreted the way they played with food which was dropped on to the floor during meal times as deriving from a natural inner urge to be active (Schulz-Benesch, 1997).

After graduating in 1896 with honours as Doctor of Medicine and Doctor of Surgery, Montessori turned her attention to children's mental health. Alongside her private medical practice, she continued her interest in medical research to find causes of nervous diseases. Montessori linked children's mental diseases with contemporary education problems as she 'felt that mental deficiency presented chiefly a pedagogical rather than mainly a medical problem' (Montessori, 1964: 31). This was significantly different to the approach taken by her contemporaries who often treated mental diseases through gymnastics or motor education. In seeking practical ways to support the children in the clinic, she discovered the writings of Jean Marc Itard and Adhered Séguin, two French doctors who had documented their experiences in the education of deficient children and the most influential of the great educators to Montessori's work (Montessori, 1964).

Jean Marc Gaspard Itard (1775–1838)

Itard is recognized to be the first to exert a seminal influence on Montessori's philosophy of education. A French physician and student of philosophy, Itard was the founder of a branch of medical science known as otiatria, concerned with diseases of the ear. He worked in Paris at the Institute for Deaf Mutes where he developed a methodical education for the sense of hearing. However, it was in 1799 when a boy, roaming wild in a forest was discovered by the villagers of Averyon, France, that Itard gained international notice.

The boy, named Victor was about 12 years of age and was described as possessing animal behaviour. Itard was invited to examine and treat Victor, who had been abandoned in the forest at birth and stripped of all human social life and culture. He possessed no language skills and walked on all fours, like the wolves he had lived with in the forest. Itard worked with him for the following eight years, using sensorial materials and the programme he had designed and used to support students with hearing difficulties. Victor remained mute and was unable to stand in an upright position but had good understanding of many words. Itard made elaborate materials, printed in capital letters, to help him recognize words and act out short written commands, but he did not progress in his skills further. When he reached 20 years of age, Itard stopped working with him. From that time on Victor regressed and died in his early 40s (Montessori, 1964; Cole, 1950; Savage L'enfant [film]). Itard chronicled his observations of Victor in *Des Primiers Development du Jeune Savage de l'Averyon* (1801), which was published in English as *The Wild Boy of Averyon* (1802).

Observation of the student

According to Montessori, Itard was 'the first educator to practise observation of his pupil in the way the sick are observed in hospitals, especially those suffering from diseases of the nervous system' (Montessori, 1964: 34). Montessori was struck by his minutely detailed descriptions of Victor's behaviour, all documented scientifically in a diary. Montessori identified this daily record as 'practically the first attempt at educational psychology' (Montessori, 1964: 34), and it clearly had a marked impact on her own evolving methodology. From her study of Itard, she reached the conclusion that Victor's education had a twofold aim, first, to provide him with a social life with other humans and, second, to provide him with an intellectual education. Victor loved and immersed himself in nature; he laughed with delight at lightning, danced in the rain and howled at the full moon, but very slowly he began to take pleasure from social experiences (Cole, 1950). Itard discarded his philosophical theories and began experimental psychology through observation, building a relationship, following his pupil's lead and establishing a repertoire of teaching methods for developing the boy's senses (Montessori, 1964: 150). Victor invariably ran since walking was unknown to him, so Itard adapted and followed behind him, observing closely, recording every facial expression and every spontaneous action Victor made. Victor's case evoked huge public and academic interest at the time.

Itard's influence on Montessori

There are elements of Itard's scientific methodology found in Montessori education. Montessori did not start with a theory but followed the natural tendencies she observed in children. Each child was closely observed as an individual case study with detailed notes and records kept of progress in development. Planned activities helped each child learn to care for himself and become prepared to enter society. Added to those planned activities were generous dosages of warmth, affection and patience, all of which helped to nurture the human spirit. The role of a Montessori teacher (or directress as Montessori preferred to call her) was to adapt to each pupil in a deliberate reversal of a traditional teacher to make learning a happy, spiritual experience.

Adhered Séguin (1812–1880)

Séguin was a Parisian teacher and later a physician of deaf-mutes who supported the Compte de Claude de Saint-Simon (1760–1825), an advocate of reconstruction of society based on loving one another (Cole, 1950: 542). William Boyd has also noted that Séguin applied the beliefs of Saint-Simon who saw 'the aim of education was not individualistic but a preparation for an ideal society' aiming for 'a community in which love would be the dominant motive of life' and 'moral education the crown of education' (Boyd, 1921: 363–5) to education. But Séguin also believed that individual sensory-motor training was essential in early education, and that the prime determinants of a successful education programme depended on both nature and nurture.

Séguin founded the first school for feeble-minded children in Paris in 1857. Mentally retarded or feeble-minded children ('mentally challenged' today) were considered unteachable. He modified Itard's experiments over a period of ten years while working with children from asylums. His work was largely documented in his *Traitement Moral et Education des Idiots* published in Paris in 1864 and in the United States in 1866. Most of his pupils were inert and helpless, spending much of the day in bed and requiring full time care (Hans, 1994: 191). The curriculum used by Séguin included practical lessons to help the development of his students. Muscular education involved lessons to help the children in feeding and clothing themselves; in teaching them to walk unassisted; in aiding them maintain equilibrium, walk upstairs and downstairs; in learning to feel muscular sensations and become independent of adults as far as they can. Muscular sensations fostered through touching and feeling objects with their hands led his students from those simple first perceptions to a more sophisticated sensory appreciation using the mind and senses. The students were accordingly more able to care for themselves, a personal growth which helped reduce the costs of their care at the school (Cole, 1950: 545–7). Lessons, given individually, were designed to be joyful and spiritual and necessarily practical, hands-on experiences. As with Itard, close individual studies of each pupil were made. Séguin designed and constructed didactic (self-correcting) materials and 'with his methods the education of idiots was actually possible' (Montessori, 1964: 37).

Séguin's influence on Montessori

Séguin's work is described in detail in his book *Treatise on Idiocy* (1864). For him, education largely depended on two things: first, the individual acting on the environment (nature) and, second, the individual responding to social relationships (nurture). His work remains a valuable resource for teachers of the deaf and special-needs children today. Montessori education incorporates a number of Séguin-related exercises. They include 'walking the line' (designed for promoting good posture) and exercises in practical life to help young children become completely or largely independent of adults (ibid.). He made a special provision for each child to develop physically, mentally and spiritually, aspects which Montessori found attractive. She designed and constructed many didactic materials for normal children's needs. Other features which she incorporated into Montessori education directly from the Séguin model were his philosophic commitments to democracy and his incorporation of democratic practices within the classroom. In Séguin's classroom, children were actively encouraged to live harmoniously together, the deliberate purpose being that such habits will have long-term consequences for the wider community. Montessori education ardently supports the identical notion, one of its larger aims being the ultimate reconstruction of a peace-loving and harmonious society.

In 1897, Montessori attended the National Medical Congress in Turin where the causes of delinquency in retarded and disturbed children were being discussed. When she began to investigate problems of delinquency, part of her investigations involved looking into the causes of deviant behaviour of criminals and to find ways to change their behaviour. It was obvious to her from observations that deviations in behaviour began at a very early age. At the time, Montessori was of the opinion that punishment 'was not a deterrent to criminality' and that a criminal 'behaved destructively because of the nature of his feelings and his reasoning' (Kramer, 1976: 74).

At the Pedagogical Congress in Turin in 1898 Montessori presented a paper, *Moral Education*, which outlined her evolving ideas on deviant behaviour in classrooms clearly showing how they were supported by the research and work of Itard and Séguin.

Her ideas of teaching Moral Education spread among doctors and teachers 'like wildfire'. The Minister of Education, Guido Baccelli, invited Montessori to present a course of lectures on the education of feeble-minded children to the teachers of Rome (Montessori, 1964: 32). These lectures aroused so much interest that the State Orthophrenic School was founded and which she directed for two years. Classes were made up of children considered to be 'hopelessly deficient' from elementary schools together with idiot children selected from the asylums (Montessori, 1964: 32). From mid-1898 to mid-1900 she taught these abnormal children from eight in the morning to seven in the evening and 'felt that the methods I had used had nothing in them peculiarly limited to the instruction of idiots'. Also, she believed the educational principles were 'more rational than those in use in normal schools' (ibid.: 31, 33; Montessori, 1939: 20). She was informed by 'the remarkable experiments of Itard and followed the methods of Séguin'. During the two years she made a great variety of new didactic materials and through their application obtained most surprising results. She found the work with 'deficient' (abnormal) children exhausting but pointed out that 'the more encouragement, comfort, love and respect given, the more we renew and invigorate the life about us' (Montessori, 1964: 36, 37). She had been guided by a deep respect and love she felt for the children, just as Séguin had described.

When some of these 'defective' children were selected and presented for an open examination, all passed while some children from State Schools failed. The deficient children had learned to read, write and count at a higher level than normal children. This surprising result led Montessori to suspect that serious deficiencies existed in the established and accepted practices in government schools (ibid.: 31, 32), and she was determined to undertake, at some time, the teaching of 'normal' children based on her principles and methods. Her methods she maintained 'contained a system of mental treatment that was very logical and superior' (Montessori, 1939: 21). After two years Montessori withdrew from working with deficient children and 'felt the need for meditation' (Montessori, 1964: 41).

Montessori travelled to London where she was presented to Queen Victoria; then on she went to Paris to study practical ways 'of educating deficients' and visit schools where new methods were being utilized. Some were using Séguin's didactic materials, most faithfully following his rules to the letter, but not one attained the spectacular results he had documented in his writings. For Montessori, the reason was simple: the materials were being used in a cold, mechanical way without the human, spiritual side of the method Séguin had injected and lacking the warmth of involvement that he had evoked from his young charges.

At this point, Montessori wished 'to make a study of normal pedagogy and the methods used for the education of normal children' even though she did not know if she would ever have the opportunity to work with normal children. She enrolled at the University of Rome in 1901. Her course of study included philosophy, experimental psychology with research into pedagogical anthropology in elementary schools (ibid.: 33, 42). The choice of subjects could have been influenced by the work and writings of her contemporary Giuseppe Sergi.

Giuseppe Sergi (1841–1936)

Sergi, a distinguished Italian anthropologist, was a lecturer at Rome University when Montessori was studying education. Her attention was attracted with his support for Scientific Pedagogy which he averred could 'lead to the science of forming man'. He ardently promoted 'the principles of a new civilization based upon education' and advocated to teachers 'the principles of a new civilization based upon education' (Montessori, 1964: 2). He wished 'to establish natural, rational methods' where teachers took 'numerous, exact and rational observations of man as an individual, principally during infancy, which is the age in which the foundations of education and culture must be laid'. Educational methods needed to be reconstructed to enable 'human regeneration', and he suggested 'a methodical study of the one to be educated . . . under the guidance of pedagogical anthropology and experimental psychology' (ibid.: 2, 3). His long-term goal was to see all men living together in harmony, a dream brought about by natural, rational methods practised by teachers who maintained regular, precise observations of children as unique individuals, 'principally during infancy, which is the age at which the foundations of education and culture are laid' (ibid.: 3). For him, the Western world's educational methodologies were in desperate need of reconstruction to bring about an overdue human regeneration. The pedagogical writings in *Edicazione ed Instruczione* were a resumé of his lectures in which he encouraged teachers to join the new movement.

Sergi's influence on Montessori

Sergi's lectures and writings about Scientific Pedagogy made a great impression on Montessori especially his educational aims for a new civilization based on 'exact observations of man as an individual'. His method was to be 'a methodical study of the one to be educated' (ibid.). There were no guidelines as to how Scientific Pedagogy should be done, but Montessori noted:

> Scientific Pedagogy has never yet been definitely constructed nor defined. It is something vague that we speak about . . . pedagogy must join with medicine was the thought of the time.
>
> (ibid.: 2, 3)

For Montessori, Scientific Pedagogy, like medicine, had to prove itself through clinical, scientific experimentation, and with her specialized medical expertise as a paediatrician with a particular interest in mental health, she determined at the first opportunity to 'make a study of normal pedagogy and the methods used for the education of normal children' (ibid.: 33, 64).

While studying pedagogical psychology and educational theory at University of Rome in 1901, Montessori became familiar with the theories and writings of Locke, Rousseau, Pestalozzi and Robert Owen (Kramer, 1976). All of these educators visualized education as a means of creating a new, ideal society, particularly Robert Owen who set out in practical ways to help his factory workers improve their education and their lifestyles resulting in their general happiness in life. In his model village infant school, at his own cotton mill in New Lanark, Scotland, these dramatic changes in the human condition became a reality (Conservation Trust, Scotland, 1997). Her studies also included philosophy and research into pedagogical anthropology in elementary schools. During that research period she carried out her own empirical studies (Müller and Schneider, 2002), taking particular notice of children sitting motionless at stationary desks and benches, remaining silent all day listening to the teacher talking. Learning was supposed to take place by rote. Children were coerced in doing what the teacher chose to do, and they were punished severely for any errors (Montessori, 1964: 21, 33, 42). She concluded that such schools were not happy places, and there simply had to be a better way for students of all ages to learn. She noted that through actual experience 'I had justified my faith in Séguin's method'. She began 'an even more thorough study of the works of Itard and Séguin . . . translated them into Italian and copied out with my own hand the writings of these men from beginning to end'. She did this 'in order that I might have time to weigh the sense of each word and read in truth the *spirit* of the author' (ibid.). On completion of the 600 page volume, she received a copy of the updated volume in English. She translated this volume into Italian with the help of an English friend (ibid.: 41, 42). On completion of her University studies in 1904, Montessori was offered the Chair in Anthropology at the University of Rome. She also continued her private practice and became an active member of the feminist and socialist movements (Standing, 1966).

It was towards the end of 1906 that Montessori was invited by Eduard Tamalo, Director General of the Association for Good Building in Rome, to open an infants' school in one of the model tenement buildings on the San Lorenzo district of Rome. Signor Tamalo wished that children from 3 years to 7 years attend school to save the new tenement properties being vandalized by unsupervised children while their parents were at work in the nearby textile factories. He offered Montessori a whole ground floor apartment which opened onto an enclosed courtyard, and another apartment within the building for a teacher. Here was her opportunity to study non-deficient children in a 'scientific' manner and she wished 'to make this school a field for scientific experimental pedagogy' with the view that 'child psychology can be established only through the method of external observation'.

Montessori pointed out that 'anthropology and psychology have never devoted themselves to the question of educating children in schools' (Montessori, 1964: 4). Her plan was to be scientific and learn from observing children whom she regarded as natural beings rather than learning from 'a body of knowledge from the past' (Butts, 1955: 177). Her aim 'as with idiot children, was to aid development of young children adapted to their entire personality' (Montessori, 1964: 45). Her method was to observe children in the way anthropologists and scientists observe natural phenomena. The controls for the experiment were a prepared environment with some didactic materials and boundaries set by the teacher. She recognized and took into consideration the variability of the individual child. She planned to study each child and keep carefully recorded observation notes of each child's development 'without clinging to any dogma about the activity of the child according to age'. She stressed the need for psychologists to 'renounce all idea of making any record of any internal states, which can be revealed only by the retrospection of the subject himself' (Montessori, 1964: 72, 73).

Was Montessori education a scientific method in 1907?

It is arguable that the roots of Montessori education date back to the sixteenth century when the beginning of modern science began to appear with a shift to human experiences and natural interests of the world. Beliefs and assumptions, according to Butts, included three particular features, namely:

1) a certainty that the *secrets of nature* could be revealed
2) that 'science' should mean what we can learn from looking at nature not a body of knowledge from the past
3) the development of scientific technique for obtaining new knowledge through:
   observation of nature
   collection of facts
   objective verification of facts
   use of mathematical formulas in the process
   application of results (Butts, 1955: 177).

Scientific Pedagogy

Scientific Pedagogy has never yet been definitely constructed or defined.

It is something vague of which we speak . . .

(Montessori, 1964: 2)

It was nature's secrets that Montessori wished to discover in her research. At the end of the nineteenth century there were no clear definitions for Scientific Pedagogy. Pioneers in education who were experimenting with making education more relevant used scientific terms. Lawson and Silver identify among those pioneers Matthew Davenport (1822) who concluded that 'education was of the nature of science' because 'it involved the study of phrenology, psychology and philosophy'. Alexander Bain (1870) defined 'education as science, and teaching as an art form from a scientific point of view which could lead to the formation of general psychology and physiological rules' (Lawson and Silver, 1973: 353). There was much discussion among academics to have education accepted as a science which meant theories and practices needed to be proved with scientific precision. Proof, at that time, required equations and statistics. But Montessori's work was not considered to be scientific at that time because it lacked such proof (Fynne, 1924). Her findings could not be presented by equations and statistics, and therefore many academics initially rejected the validity of her work.

Montessori and the First Children's House

2

The first Casa dei Bambini became a laboratory of psychology.

(Montessori, 1967a: 49)

The school opened in January, 1907, at 58 Via dei Masi, Rome, and thus began Montessori's experiments. Her observation notes were recorded over two years and first published in *Scientific Pedagogy as Applied to Child Education in the Children's House* (Montessori, 1964: 42, 43) and in 1912 in over 20 languages including English. In all her future work with normal children, Montessori was to draw on her observations and first-hand experiences with abnormal children. She noted,

> My intention was to keep in touch with the researches of others, but to make myself independent of them, preceding to my work without preconceptions of any kind.
>
> (Montessori, 1964: 72)

The first experiment

In this first Casa dei Bambini (Children's House), Montessori prepared the environment with a few small tables and chairs along with toys. Forty children between the ages of 3 and 7 were enrolled and put in the care of Candida Nuccitelli, who had done some teacher training, and an assistant who had completed some elementary studies. Senora Nuccitelli was given clear instructions that the only time she had to intervene was 'to check whatever offends or annoys others or whatever tends towards rough or ill-bred acts' because 'we cannot know the consequences of stifling a spontaneous action when the child is just beginning to be active: perhaps we will stifle life itself' (ibid.: 87). Everything else was to be permitted and observed.

There were no guidelines as to how Scientific Pedagogy should be done, since in Montessori's words 'anthropology and psychology have never devoted themselves to the question of educating children in schools' (ibid.: 4). To her, 'the fundamental principle of Scientific Pedagogy must be the *liberty of the pupil*', and if Scientific Pedagogy 'is to be born then schools must permit free, natural manifestations of the children' and the method she would adapt would be **'observation of free children'** (ibid.: 5, 28). In the new Casa dei Bambini, children were treated with respect, and great consideration was given to the physical and mental health of each child.

What was new in the Montessori method?

Practical life materials for motor education

Montessori began to introduce practical life materials which were intended for motor education. They were similar to those she had used in the asylum to help those children care for their environment and personal needs, and designed to help the development of each child's sense of order, coordination and independence. All were introduced to each child individually through silent demonstration, just as Séguin had done with deaf-mute children. Silent demonstration allowed a normal child to concentrate on the activity and not to be distracted or confused by language. The practical life activities included:

- Caring for the environment using specially made child-sized household materials. Tasks such as mopping the floor or verandah encouraged the use and development of large muscles.
- Caring for pets and plants in the garden. Preparing food for pets and weeding and watering plants in the garden cultivated a sense of responsibility.
- Preparing food, setting the table and serving lunch for the whole group, encouraging shared experiences and introducing young children to the social life within the classroom.
- Learning about personal hygiene, the importance of washing hands and washing themselves.

Montessori noted how calmness of the nervous system and concentration were developed as children polished brass objects or scrubbed the floor. Many practical life activities, such as buttoning and bow-tying exercises were designed 'to help the development of co-ordinated movements of the fingers' (Montessori, 1964: 145) especially the coordination between the thumb and the first two fingers. Basic as these skills were, Montessori's hidden aim was that mastery of such skills allowed children to become more independent of adults. She emphasized that all free movement was synonymous with 'spontaneous development' (Montessori, 1964: 230), and observed that it was through movements of the hand that the young children made their growing knowledge most evident. By 1939 Montessori wrote about 'the intelligence of the hand', and about how the hand was responsible for all of civilization as it was 'companion of the mind'. The hands, she averred were 'connected to mental life' (psychomotor), and so 'the study of a child's psychological development must be closely bound up with the hand's activities, which are stimulated by his mind' (Montessori, 1967a: 151, 152).

Montessori differentiated between motor education and muscular education (gymnastics). Muscular education was 'to aid the normal development of physiological movements (such as walking, breathing and speech) including walking the line', as Séguin had first suggested for the development of equilibrium, poise and graceful, coordinated movements. Muscular education improved circulation and thereby health. Through observation of children and their movements, Montessori designed a kind of jungle-gym to allow children to move along sideways and kick their legs freely, the variety of exercises 'tending to establish co-ordination of movements' (ibid.: 138, 141–4).

Discovery of silence – control of movement

Quite by chance Montessori discovered that children loved silence. She met a mother with her sleeping baby in the courtyard. She took the child and invited the woman into the classroom. The children ran to meet Montessori but did not touch her 'through respect for the little one I held'. The children sat on the floor, but, no one had yet spoken for the child still slept. Finally, Montessori whispered, 'I have brought you a little teacher.' There were surprised glances and laughter. 'A little teacher, yes, because none of you know how to be as quiet as she does.' All the children changed positions and became quiet. Montessori whispered, 'Yet no one holds his limbs and feet as quiet as she.' Everyone gave closer attention to the position of limbs and feet. The lesson continued until there was *great silence.* They became conscious of being still, and when they moved they walked on tip toes. From this experience Montessori developed games of silence, for self-control and the perfection of muscle control. Children can use 'their will power for the purposes of action and restraint of action' (Montessori, 1939: 262).

Sensorial education: The aim of sensorial materials

One of the most important features of the Children's House was the sensorial materials. Two millennia before Montessori, Aristotle had informed us that 'everything we know is first in the senses', but it was Montessori who made clear to educators that the senses were the most neglected in the learning process. She modified Itard's sensory materials used by deficient children (Montessori 1964: 169). Each child was introduced to each piece of material individually. He was invited to observe a silent demonstration of a piece of material, or was given a three-period lesson for some other materials, and only then was he allowed to work with the materials himself. The rewards with these self-instructive materials lay in 'waiting for the spontaneous reaction of children'. It was experimental psychology at work and from it she hoped that psychology would 'be able to draw conclusions from pedagogy and not vice versa' (ibid.: 167). For Montessori, it was the materials that made education possible with 'deficient' children, but normal children taught themselves using self-correcting didactic materials. Montessori education was based on the spontaneous interest of each child, therefore Montessori maintained, 'collective lessons are of secondary importance (for children 3–6 years) and have been abolished by us' (ibid.: 108).

Attention and concentration

In 1890, William James had spoken of 'that extreme mobility of attention with which we are all familiar in children . . . and any education which should improve this faculty would be *the education par excellence*' (James, 1890: 404). The aim of each piece of sensorial material was to focus the child's attention. Every child was introduced to each piece of material individually. He was free to choose any piece of the material he had been introduced to and work with it for as long as he wished. It was to be replaced by the child exactly where it had been found on the shelf, ready to be used by the next child who wished to work with the same material. Every exercise required the child to concentrate on the task at hand while developing control over his body and will. The final step in these activities (except the colour activities) was to blind-fold the child, depriving him of the sense of sight. Montessori found that the deprivation of sight aroused even deeper interest in the activity and sharpened the child's sense of touch to complete the activity. She noted that when a child became fully focused on a piece of material his nervous system became relaxed and calmness took over his behaviour. This behaviour change was to have a profound influence on Montessori and marked the commencement of what she later was to term the process of 'normalization'. The discovery that behaviour change accompanied increased concentration was a by-product of the learning conditions in the first Children's House in 1907, and when the self-teaching sensorial materials were introduced to the children, they became less attracted to dolls and toys (ibid.: 171). The work cycle brought inner joy and satisfaction to the child on completion of the task. The number of times a child repeated each exercise was carefully recorded because 'in order to repeat there must first be an idea to be repeated. A mental grasp of an idea is indispensable to the beginning of repetition' (ibid.: 224). It was repetition of an action that led to mental development (ibid.: 224, 358). The child stopped repeating the action when his inner development was complete. In the first Casa dei Bambini, Montessori observed a child repeat a cylinder block exercise 43 times. She was able to show repeatedly that young children do have long attention spans provided they choose their work and are interested in what they are doing. It was important that the directress did not interrupt the child during this work as she needed 'to allow his actions to follow the laws of time differing from our own' (ibid.: 358). It was 'an erroneous idea that the end to be obtained was the completion of the action' because it was 'attention, comparison, judgement, intellectual gymnastics that aid formation of the intellect' (ibid.: 158, 360). When the child concentrated attention on the task at hand, it could lead to 'mental explosion which delights the child' as he 'makes discoveries in the world about him' (ibid.: 361). To Montessori, the external sign of learning was the joy of the child. She concluded that with repetition the child perfected psycho-sensory processes.

Order of the mind

Some children, Montessori observed, became agitated if materials or objects were not in exact order. She was strongly of the opinion that an orderly classroom helped each child maintain an orderly mind. The didactic material for the development of the senses was grouped to a definite *quality* such as 'colour, shape, dimensions, sound, surface texture, weight, temperature' (ibid.: 119). The series of objects 'will bring one quality only into prominence' so *isolation* of 'a single quality in the material' was necessary. Each piece of didactic material possessed four characteristics which were: control of error, aesthetics, activity and limits. These qualities were common to all materials for development within the prepared environment and indirectly helped to prepare each child for later experiences. Although children were free to choose any material they wished, Montessori noted that each child chose 'any object which at that moment corresponds with his most acute needs for action' as 'certain flowers attract insects' (Montessori, 1967a: 122). This suggested that each child had a limited choice, because he was always guided by and followed nature. Also, Montessori found that children were attracted to any object which could be moved, was able to be made and unmade, or displaced and replaced. Such an object 'made prolonged occupation possible' (ibid.: 123). In contrast she found, a beautiful toy, an attractive picture, an interesting story could arouse interest but if the children could only look and listen and not touch the object, their interest soon passed. The environment must satisfy children's love of activity by containing objects which children 'can move, use and put back and then the attraction of surroundings is inexhaustible' (ibid.). She insisted the material must be limited, pointing out that it was wrong to think that children who had the most toys and received much help were the best developed, 'instead, the confused multitude of things raises more chaos in his mind and oppresses him with discouragement' (ibid.: 124). She stated that the child's mind from birth was an unconscious absorbent mind, and the thousands of impressions 'taken in' resulted in the mind being in chaos by 3 years (ibid.: 118). The Montessori sensorial materials helped the child *order the mind* because the materials were limited. He became 'passionately attached to these things which bring order to the chaos accumulated within him'. There was only one of each piece of material within the classroom. The limits 'enable the child to reduce his mind to order' (ibid.: 124).

Errors and self-correction

Didactic materials were designed so the child could identify and self-correct. This meant that errors became a private experience, because only the child concerned (and an observant teacher) knew a mistake had been made. Errors could provide valuable educational experiences by allowing a child to exercise his intelligence in any number of trials. Control of error required the mind to be prepared and children had to apply reasoning power, resulting in 'growing exactitude and intelligence that could distinguish small differences' (ibid.: 122). The materials in the prepared environment were designed 'to make control of mistakes an easy matter'. When a child confidently performed an activity correctly every time, that piece of material became of no further use to him and he would no longer choose that activity. Self-correction led the child to concentrate his attention on the comparisons of the various pieces: 'the psycho-sensory exercise lies in the comparison' (Montessori, 1964: 171). Sensorial materials were designed specifically to attract each child's attention to one definite quality such as dimension, colour, sound, texture, weight or temperature.

Freedom (nature): The first principle of Montessori education

Freedom was and is the first principle of Montessori education. The idea of liberty itself was not new because 'Rousseau and others had suggested vague notions of liberty of children', but these educators were more interested in social liberty which 'did not inform education' (ibid.: 15). The type of liberty Montessori was suggesting, that of freeing the child's spirit (mind), was unknown in education. For this, children required a stress free environment. She was calling for *change*. What was needed was a quiet revolution within classrooms. She declared that 'the principle of slavery still pervades pedagogy' and 'proof of slavery was to be seen in stationary desks and benches' which were there 'to repress the movement' of children to a state of immobility. Children's health was at risk. They needed physical freedom for their bodies and muscles to develop normally, and for good circulation so bones did not become deformed. Montessori had much to say about the school desk with bench.

Montessori noted the desk with fixed bench was designed so the child could not stand at his work but could sit only in an erect position in an effort to prevent the curvature of the spine but made it possible for the child to become humpbacked because the vertebral column bent under the yoke of the school.

Science had perfected an instrument of slavery' (ibid.: 17–19) and she suggested 'a rational method of combating spinal curvature is to change the form of work, with children no longer obliged to remain for so many hours a day in a harmful position. It is liberty which the school needs, not the mechanism of the bench' (ibid.: 19). To Montessori, freedom to move while working was essential for good mental health because 'Movement was synonymous with psychic development' (Montessori, 1909: 230). Montessori recognized the need for physical movement for psychical development, and the need for inner joy and happiness for good mental health She had shown the importance of refining large movements but it was the **hand**, working with the didactic materials which brought about learning. By 1939 Montessori wrote about 'the intelligence of the hand and about how it was responsible for all civilization as it was 'connected to mental life' (psychomotor) and so 'the study of a child's psychological developmentmust be closely bound with the hand's activities, which are stimulated by the mind' (Montessori, 1939: 151–2). Her practical life activities and sensorial didactic materials made such a study of the hand possible.

The major concern for Montessori was that the physical treatment of children in schools depressed each child's spirit (ibid.: 20). Punishments, which 'were an aid to the master to ensure immobility', also helped to depress the spirit. Joy and happiness were necessities of life and she saw the free spirit as being 'a given' to human beings. She observed that schools generally were not happy places. There was a need for a *new* school where each child could grow healthy and become happy. In the first Casa dei Bambini dual desks were replaced by light weight tables and small movable chairs. There were no punishments. Montessori maintained that freedom of the spirit was the birth right of every child.

What did Montessori mean by freedom?

The freedom enjoyed by the children in the first Casa dei Bambini was not a 'laissez-faire' atmosphere which could lead to aggression and confusion. In Montessori education there were carefully defined boundaries. The children were allowed freedom with responsibility which involved *respect* for everything within the environment. *Responsibility* meant:

- Children were to respect and care for:
  - the didactic materials and the furnishings within the environment
  - the belongings of others.

- Children were to show respect for others (children and adults) by:
  - becoming conscious of others' needs and feelings
  - considering others before themselves through good manners
  - allowing space for others to work in peace
  - not interrupting others
  - recognising the rights of others.
  - Children were to gain self-respect through:
  - success, which brought inner joy
  - awareness of the outcomes of their own actions
  - adapting socially to a group
  - being empowered and responsible for their own learning.

Montessori education instilled respect in children with free spirits, recognized the need for movement, the need of respect for the environment and the rights of others, the need for self-respect and the need to be responsible for one's own actions and one's own learning. Crucially, a responsible sense of freedom was encouraged, as opposed to libertarian freedom which allowed an individual to ignore the rights of others. Within a Montessori environment there was a socially controlled freedom which relied upon social constructions. Freedom had as its limit the group itself, because the child was not free to do as he pleased but free to become master of himself and able to work independently of the teacher.

What did Montessori discover from her observation of free children?

> At most, I have been the children's interpreter, through observation.
>
> (Montessori, 1973c: 4)

Psychologists at the beginning of the twentieth century based much of their work on 'animal behaviour and adult responses to psychological analyses' (ibid.: 67). As a result, children were treated in the same manner as animals when their responses were either rewarded or punished. Psychologists and teachers believed that children learned when correct responses were rewarded. Any wrong response was punished, and negative behaviour was repressed to escape punishment. Clearly, Montessori's study of each individual child in a classroom setting was entirely different from the clinical study of laboratory animals, with conclusions transferred to animals at large. Each Montessori experiment 'refrain[s] from inciting reactions depending on the will of the experimenter . . . it offers freely chosen activity by the children' (Montessori, 1967a: vii). The principle of free choice was extremely important in Montessori education since it was dependent on the will of the child, not a common fact in school situations at that time. Children's responses to freely chosen activities in the Children's House were neither rewarded nor punished, and children's spirits were never repressed.

Observation of free active children in a classroom setting in 1907 was a new concept in education. It had never been considered before by educators. Indeed, in Montessori's view it was impossible to make observations in public schools, because during her course at University when she carried out empirical studies, she noted 'children were like dead butterflies pinned to place' (Müller and Schneider, 2003). They sat immobile listening to the teacher, and they were all expected to learn 'barren meaningless knowledge' all in the same time by rote and to obey every command of the teacher. Children were 'repressed in spontaneous expression of personality, like dead things' (Montessori, 1964: 14). Always, they were treated as a group and referred to as 'the class'.

Discovery of tendencies

> What is called the Montessori Method resulted from the discovery of tendencies.
>
> (Montessori Course, London, 1933)

When Montessori began observing free children acting within her prepared environment in 1907 they revealed their *natural* tendencies to her. They *tended to*:

a) select materials that attracted them
b) concentrate and become calmer
c) choose what to do rather than wait for set tasks
d) work with amazing concentration
e) repeat an activity they were interested in
f) be orderly
g) prefer work to play
h) prefer didactic materials to toys
i) refuse rewards
j) require no punishments
k) enjoy silence
l) possess a sense of personal dignity
m) become independent (Montessori, 1964)

The observations of these natural *tendencies* which the free children revealed to Montessori founded the principles of Montessori education which was truly based on children rather than theory. As a result, there was never a gap between the practice (which came first) and her theory (which was developed later).

Another principle of Montessori education is 'studying the child before educating him' (ibid.: 15). This had been established by Itard's study of one boy, but Montessori proposed to study all 40 children individually before their education began. This was a new concept in education. She wrote that it was 'toward *single* individuals, one by one observed, that education must direct itself' (ibid.: 104). She kept detailed notes on every child and individual education developed within the Montessori environment. It was based on *free choice and interest* of each child. Montessori education was the first to introduce the concept of individual learning which was 'developed upon systematic individual work . . . its basis – individual interest' (Montessori Course, India, 1942). Other educators were to follow with individualized programmes but none offered free choice and interests of pupils.

Although clinical observation was one of medicine's major tools for diagnosis, Montessori's observations of each individual child in a classroom setting 'were not considered to be scientific' in the educational world (Fynne, 1924: 321). She was following the observational practice of Jean Itard whom she regarded as 'the founder of scientific pedagogy' (Montessori, 1967a: 21), and so her *educational psychology* 'was the carefully recorded observations of the subject and the study of development' (Montessori, 1964: 73). She made careful notes about each child's development from her observations. As a result of this it was unnecessary to test children, because she already knew what each child could do. No testing and no examinations meant children were stress free in the classroom environment. They were relaxed and their mental health was enhanced.

Once, when questioned about how to observe children, Montessori responded:

When I am in the midst of children I do not think of myself as a scientist, a theoretician. When I am with children I am a nobody . . . this enables me to see things one would miss if one was somebody, little things, simple but very precious *truths*. (Montessori, 1972: 101)

Observation and practice before theory

Montessori maintained that she did not begin with a theory but an observation. She insisted 'we proceeded starting with the child himself' but the 'pedagogical world is guided by human logic when Nature has other laws' (Montessori, 1967a: 67). She noted that 'while psychologists seek a method of education to suit their theory, we seek a psychological theory to suit our method' (ibid.: 25). She always took her lead from children. In other words, she followed Nature. It was only after her observations of children using her materials that Montessori formulated a psychological theory. *Practice came first, theory later.* At a Course in 1946, she made the following statement:

I have never affirmed anything that I have reasoned in my mind because if I did it would just be a theory of no importance, just be a matter of opinion not a serious statement. Serious statements must come from observations of development – *the truth*. (Montessori Course, London, 1946)

For all interested in the welfare of children, especially those working in schools, she called for great *change*.

Social relationships (nurture)

Our aim in education is twofold, biological and social.

(Montessori, 1964: 215)

Until the Casa dei Bambini opened in 1907, the common relationship between teacher and children was established on the incorrect presumption of the teacher's superiority and her right to dominate the child. The social relationship found in a Montessori environment in 1907 was one where

> in the psychological realm of relationship between teacher and child, the
> teacher's part and its techniques are analogous to those of the valet, they
> are to serve, and to serve well : to serve the spirit. This is something new,
> especially in the education field. (Montessori, 1964: 256)

The child could have been viewed as superior, but the role of this *new* Montessori teacher was to help children to become independent, self-reliant, masters of themselves. The teacher relinquished her power by not forcing her will on children, by not selecting everything the children had to do all day, but she did direct and help the development of the whole child, *a personality*. In Montessori's own words, the teacher 'must be as one inspired by a deep worship of life . . . respect while she observes with human interest, the development of the child's life' (ibid.: 104). She was able to help the child develop his will by empowering him to choose his own experiences in the prepared environment. Montessori children were encouraged to think and act for themselves (Montessori, 1967a: 257).

A new teacher

The new humane teacher Montessori described treated children with respect as fellow human beings with social rights. She was to treat each child in the manner she wished to be treated herself by others. She was no longer a figure of authority nor did she allow children to do as they pleased, but the friendly social conditions brought joy and happiness which Montessori always referred to as the *keys* to life and noted that 'the educator must be interested in the development of life' (Montessori, 1964: 104).

To Montessori, *relationships* were the very *crux of education*. There was respect and trust between students and teacher (ibid.: 13), and students were encouraged to cooperate and help each other. The teacher worked with every child individually every day, and so they grew to *know and trust* each other. A Montessori teacher was to respect, trust and, in addition, love every child (ibid.: 12). There were different levels of love. The first was the personal care of the parent and the second was not personal, not material but was a spiritual relationship practised by the teacher.

Social justice for children in the classroom

A major concern for Montessori was that the physical treatment of children in schools depressed each child's spirit which affected 'spontaneous psychic development' (ibid.: 230). In the Casa dei Bambini, children could move freely and talk to each other, their rights as human beings respected. In a sense, they were suddenly emancipated by the unprecedented conditions of their school environment. These children had no fear of tests, exams, failure or being corrected frequently because they did not experience any of these features. The aim of the materials was that each child would experience success. For Montessori, success was an important issue of simple justice. She sought freedom of the mind and good mental health brought about by anxiety-free learning conditions within the classroom environment

Children's social rights were recognized by Montessori in 1907, but as she noted 30 years later, there was 'no recognition of the rights of children in history . . . the word education was synonymous with punishment . . . and there was no one to defend them (Montessori, 1978: 236). Justice in the classroom, for Montessori, was 'to try to ensure that every child shall make the best of himself' by giving 'every human being the help he needs to bring about his fullest spiritual stature' (Montessori, 1967a: 285). Montessori children experienced social justice at 3 years of age. The issue of justice for children continued, and the plight of children was so important to Montessori that she fought constantly for their rights and encouraged parents to do the same from the beginning of the twentieth century. Ultimately she took the issue to the world in 1951 presenting a paper for UNESCO titled 'The Rights of Children' (Kramer, 1976). It was by no means a politicizing of children. At present, well-known figures such as Hilary Clinton, a Montessori mother (Olaf, 2001), continue to call for Rights for Children.

Montessori's first principle of Freedom with responsibilities brought many new living conditions into the classroom. It was important for good mental health, and it allowed her to make observations of free children. Children revealed their natural tendencies which became the principles of Montessori education. She discovered how children were able to be in control of every muscle through their love of silence. Freedom promoted social relationships between children and a humane teacher, and to Montessori, relationships were the crux of education. The humane teacher provided for social justice within the classroom where children had rights.

Critics and supporters

Montessori made radical changes within the first *Casa dei Bambini* in 1907. Her approach was to act and do what was possible by beginning with practical action and demonstrating how changes could be made within classrooms. Her actions were widely criticized by academics at the time. However, her approach evolved and continues to flourish today.

In the 1950s it was still uncommon in non-Montessori schools for children to be respected or to be empowered to choose their own experiences. It was not until about 1960 with the publication of A. S. Neill's *Summerhill* (1960), a school where there was complete freedom with no adult restrictions, that a wave of writings began to appear by new humanistic educators including Holt's blistering critique of the ways schools can destroy the minds and emotions of young children in *How Children Fail* (1964) (Gage and Berliner, 1979: 558, 560).

Advocates of humanistic approaches to education in the 1960s held the belief that 'the learner should take more responsibility for determining what is to be learned and become more self-directing and independent'. It required 'a change in the teacher's status from superior to the student to being equal to the student . . . the choice of subject matter is considered to be a student's right' (ibid.: 559).

It was in 1980 that Shelly Phillips, a supporter of Montessori education, wrote 'surprisingly few genuinely regard children as being of the human species and as persons one can take seriously as suffering hurt and damage to feelings' (Phillips, 1980: 10, 11). So more than 20 years after educators began to write about humanistic education and 70 years after Montessori first put it into practice, little had changed in most classrooms. Teachers were still authoritarian figures. However, Phillips commented that teachers were 'clutching at a new style of teaching described as authoritative' (ibid.: 11). This article described the old authoritarian approach of discipline as emphasising teachers' rights while the permissive approach emphasised children's rights where 'the freedom is a way of avoiding responsibility for the child's development'. The new authoritative approach sought 'a balance between the duties and rights of teachers and the duties and rights of children' (ibid.: 12). Phillips discussed findings of psychologists in the 1980s and they were exactly what Montessori had considered to be the responsible way of treating children but now went under the new name of 'authoritative'. Phillips continued, 'the psychologists seem totally unaware of the similarities between the methods they employ and those of Montessori while the teachers who used the authoritative approach were quite uconscious that the ghost of Montessori hangs over them' (ibid.: 13, 14). It was this authoritative approach that Montessori had found to be helpful in forming amicable social relationships within the classroom nearly 80 years earlier.

Relationship to current issues

Multiple literacies

Today, justice, equality and democracy are included with learning to read and write as literacy skills. According to Street (1995: 21), children are to be helped to become literate in today's world and so 'free them from oppression and ignorance'. Lankshear, Gee, Knobel and Searle (1997) are in favour of Critical Literacy which elevates emancipation of oppressed people 'to a universal avocation' (in Muspratt et al., 1997: 151). Robinson (1994) laments that 'the use of the word oppression is now so broad it includes almost everyone who suffers in some way through exploitation or existential anxiety' (in Castells et al., 1999: 21). Critical pedagogy examines what is taken for granted, wishing to establish a project of emancipation and create a just society (Castells et al., 1999).

Humanistic education

From observation and personal experience the authoritative approach is found commonly in classrooms today. Humanistic relationships are seen in many Early Childhood classrooms and children move about the rooms freely but most remain teacher centred, in the manner prescribed by Fröebel, with teachers in control of timetables and curriculum. There are many 'open' classrooms and some multi-age classrooms, but many teachers are transferred into these 'new' classrooms without them having any interest in changing their methods of teaching. Two teachers can find themselves team teaching; in an open area classroom but instead of providing individualized work, one teacher takes the whole group for certain subjects while the other teacher prepares or marks work. There is no advantage for the students in the simple change of the architecture of an open classrooms Teachers need to change their teaching methods by providing for the individual needs of children in their care.

Older children in high schools can find themselves in 'open area' designed classrooms but still have an authoritarian teacher conducting whole-class teaching. But there are large numbers of teachers who do empower their students, who adapt an authoritative stance and apply some individualized work, but pressures of time and curriculum do not allow children much choice. Advocates of whole language hold the belief of humanistic educators, and a status of equality in classrooms can be found between pupils and teacher. Here you can find children able to choose work that interests them along with a teacher willing to follow their interests. There are many teachers who are naturally humanistic towards their students.

In every Montessori classroom world-wide, for more than a century, the status of equality between teachers and students of all ages from 2½ years to 18 years is established. Montessori children are treated with the same respect attributed to adults. Montessori children continue to be respected and trusted to follow their own interests, empowered to teach themselves and are acknowledged as active learners.

Relevance of freedom, emancipation and equality in schools

In more recent years, attention has been focussed on the need for freedom and equality in schools. Divorkin (1978) sees justice in schools in the manner Montessori applied it. He makes a distinction also between treating people equally and treating them as equals asserting that 'when we treat people equally everyone gets the same regardless of need. When we treat people as equals, the claims of each are considered whether or not this leads to unequal treatment. Most people agree that the needy should get more' (in Corson, 1993: 30). In practice, Montessori did treat children as equals giving each child the help needed to succeed. It was Farganis (1975), with a deep interest in Critical Social Science, who called for emancipation of all concerned in schools, but the problem of how to establish that emancipation remains unresolved in his model (Carr and Kemmis, 1986). Montessori education has shown for over a century how children can be freed at the same time as they are guided into making sound decisions which are right and just for the whole group.

Brian Street (1995: 21) 'wishes children to become literate and so free them from oppression and ignorance because of lack of literary skills'. The skills required today include more than learning to read and write. Montessori children learn to become independent of adults at 3 years and learn the social graces and cultural expectations of their society. In 1992, Ken Goodman pointed out that whole language teachers 'seek to free the minds and creative energies of pupils for the greatest gains in their intellectual, physical and social development' (Courts, 1997: 110). Advocates of whole language, a holistic approach of education, continue to develop its belief system, in which many beliefs agree with Montessori principles. Colin Lankshear and Michele Knobel are in favour of Critical Literacy which elevates emancipation, the struggles of oppressed people, 'to a universal avocation' (Muspratt et al., 1997: 151). Children remain part of the struggle. Ramon A. Serrano, an academic from a working class background, maintains that 'school oppression leads to gang formations' and that 'the path of freedom' for these children is 'through education and graduation' (Edelsky, 1999: 226, 232). Paul Willis (1997) points out that in this age of globalization those who have only 'their manual labour power to live by or sell' will discover that there is a 'global oversupply of labour'. He also states that 'no one really imagines any more that schools are about emancipation for the working class' (Castells et al., 1999: 139).

Postmodernists focus on oppression of minority groups while critical pedagogy, which examines what is taken for granted in society and social life, wishes to establish a project of emancipation and create a just society (ibid.: 21, 31). Antonia Darder sees it as a pedagogy of conflict 'normally viewed as an attempt to radically reform school' with students and teachers 'actively confronting a dominant, domineering society' which she claims is 'likely to stay in the world of academic publications' (Courts, 1997: 22, 23).

Take note, Montessori's approach in 1907 was to act and do what was possible by beginning with practice and demonstrating how changes could be made, and not through confrontation and critique. More than 90 years later Carol Edelsky maintained that educators 'need to analyse, not just complain about or to feel oppressed by our actions', and she suggested that we 'transform ourselves and our classroom or schools' (Edelsky, 1999: 145, 315) which complies with the position taken by Montessori in 1907. Further, she points out that many children today 'need freedom and responsibility which is often withheld in schools', yet children often have many responsibilities outside of school which researchers could investigate (ibid.: 336).

Relevance of observation

Observation of children today is a respected method for classroom research. It became respectable when the findings of Jean Piaget's observations were published in English in the 1960s. Most of his observations were of his own three children yet they had a great impact on the curriculum development in the United States, United Kingdom and Australia even though there was a huge gap between his theories and practice. Piaget began as a student and supporter of Montessori education, and when comparisons are made between their theories, it is not surprising that many similarities can be found. The greatest difference is that in Montessori education there is no gap between theory and practice because Montessori began with practice. Piaget never attempted to put his theory into practice.

Modern school furniture

Authorities today tend to support Montessori's recommendations about school furniture because it still causes health problems. Research by Straker (1999), senior lecturer in ergonomics at Curtain University of Technology, has found that children are especially vulnerable to physical disorders caused by inappropriate furniture. His research has found that the boom of computers in classrooms has not been accompanied by proper ergonomic furniture. Cole (1999) reports that an American study has shown that the introduction of adjustable computer furniture has led to significant improvements in children's posture. Some published evidence suggests that the use of computers in schools could result in health problems for a whole generation, and the costs to replace furniture in every Council would amount to millions of dollars as well as the costs of future litigation.

Opportunities for further research

The following questions might be elaborated upon in further research:

> How free are children in schools today?
> How do teachers handle deviant behaviour?
> Do teachers encourage self-disciple? How?
> How much respect is given by teachers to students?
> How much respect is given by students to teachers?

All special features of Montessori education are topics for further research.

Learning to write and read

The introduction of writing and reading

By the middle of 1907 the children who attended the first Children's House were demanding 'to be taught to read and write' (Montessori, 1964: 267). Initially Montessori refused because of contemporary and deep-seated thinking that 'it was necessary to begin as late as possible the teaching of reading and writing' (ibid.: 267). She relented, however, when the illiterate mothers pleaded with her to teach their children to read and write. 'If you teach them to read and write, they soon will learn and spare them the great fatigue in the elementary school', the mothers begged (ibid.: 268). These parents made an enduring impression on Montessori and the incident was another seminal period in her own personal experience.

An experiment – seeking a rational method to teaching writing, 1907

As early as 1898 Montessori concluded that Itard and Séguin had not found 'any rational method through which writing can be learned' (ibid.: 246). Seguin's writing experiments were based on the formation of capital letters and geometry, and as a result, handwriting became a long and tedious process, which produced poor results.

Montessori decided that a more rational and logical method was needed 'based essentially on articulate language' (ibid.: 310). From her direct observations of infants, Montessori maintained that spoken language, a natural function, began at birth through the child's absorbent mind. The whole process engaged physical and psychological processes. Every infant created his mother tongue by himself, through his own efforts, beginning with an isolated sound which his hearing apprehended. By 6 months he was able to articulate syllables. Intentional words appeared at about 1 year and syntax was in place at 2 years when the average child showed that he could use every part of speech correctly. Montessori emphasized that language development (identical for all children) was not taught but was natural and spontaneous following fixed laws of nature (Montessori, 1967a: 111). Montessori's detailed notes show the development of the mechanics of language, 'a necessary antecedent of the higher psychic activities which are to utilise it' (ibid.: 312). At the same time she noted that there was also a direct link between thought and language. 'Spoken language', she declared, 'begins with the child when the word pronounced by him signifies an idea' (ibid.: 314). From her own case studies she was able to show that infants had ideas long before they could speak, and that an infant's thought was fixed by one word – a *noun*. She was convinced that a child had a greater understanding of language than his power to use language, with 'a great disproportion between the powers of expression and the inner work the child was doing' (Montessori, 1938: 113). She cited as an example an observation of one eighteen-month-old child barely able to articulate a single word who 'could follow the whole drift of a long conversation' (Montessori, 1978: 69).

Montessori's investigations began by visiting mainstream classrooms where she discovered that written language was 'taught without any consideration of its relation to articulate language' (Montessori, 1964: 310). She saw clearly a link between handwriting and spoken language and began observing children, focusing on the writer not the writing, 'the subject not the object' (ibid.: 260). It was to mark a stark break with the past. She reflected that writers made two movements – first, one that manipulated the instrument for writing; second, one in which the form of the letters are reproduced. She decided to begin introducing writing to the children in September of 1907 when children in the state system resumed after the summer break. That would enable her to compare the progress of the two groups of children from an equal start. There was a setback to Montessori's plan in mid-1907 when she was unable to find someone to make a replica of a wooden alphabet she had used successfully with deficient children in 1898. In desperation she began to cut out letters from sandpaper and was to discover that these sandpaper letters acted as a guide for children to control movement as they traced a letter shape. She wrote, 'If I had been rich, I would have had that beautiful but barren alphabet of the past' (ibid.: 269).

The accidental discovery of sandpaper letters involved major modifications to Montessori's original method using a solid wooden alphabet, and as she worked cutting out sandpaper letters 'there unfolded before my mind, a clear vision of a method, in all its completeness, so simple that it made me smile' (ibid.). She decided on three pieces of material for children learning to write and read. First, there were metal insets. Her observations showed that writers made two movements – manipulating the instrument for writing and reproducing the form of the letters. Working with a pencil and the insets would provide each child the opportunity to perfect both pencil grip and pencil control. Second, there were sandpaper letters to utilise the sense of touch (sometimes used with eyes closed to enhance the child's sensory experience) to begin to learn the letter forms. Third, there was a movable alphabet of loose single letters which would allow each child to compose words for himself. Montessori trialled these materials, her aim being to increase the child's receptive and expressive language abilities through auditory, visual, cognitive experiences and activities. These especially designed materials allowed each child to teach himself to read silently with understanding. The processes were recorded in minute detail so anyone could implement the correct procedures to gain the same successful results.

Metal insets

Montessori began with metal insets which were geometric shapes placed within a metal square frame. Taking one inset and its frame, a square piece of paper the exact size of the frame and two contrasting coloured pencils, she demonstrated in silence the use of one frame to one child who then repeated the exercise. As he worked, he was preparing his muscular mechanisms for holding and manipulating the pencil by drawing parallel lines within the geometric figure, trying not to pass outside the contour. Montessori noted that by filling one figure, the child repeated the same movement of manipulation which would have filled ten copy book pages. The child showed no boredom or fatigue because he chose to do the filling in and so doing 'established exactly the muscular co-ordination for the management of the instrument of writing' (Montessori, 1964: 174).

Observation of children using insets revealed a developmental progression. The lines tended to go less outside the enclosed line until they became perfectly contained in the outline, and the strokes changed from short and confused to longer and more parallel, extending from one side to the other. Drawing parallel lines from left to right not only helped pencil control but also had a calming, therapeutic effect on the child. With practice, Montessori wrote, 'the child became master of the pencil as muscular mechanism is established' (ibid.: 273). Each child acquired a collection or portfolio of the inset designs which 'grew more and more perfect and of which they are very proud' (ibid.: 275). Such preparation of the hand for handwriting is unique to Montessori education.

Sandpaper letters

Sandpaper letters (all as cursive lower-case letter shapes) were used to introduce the alphabet to children. These auto-didactic materials comprised the 26 lower case letters made from the finest sandpaper mounted on smooth cards with vowels glued on blue card and consonants on red card. While the children perfected control of the pencil using the metal insets, the sandpaper letters were introduced to continue the natural development of articulate language, beginning with a vocal sound, not the alphabetic name of a letter. That sandpaper letter (a symbol) represented the vocal sound, and it became a direct link with spoken language.

A three-period lesson

Children were always introduced to two letters (lower case), as different in shape and sound as possible, for example, *n* and *d* were introduced to a child using the three-period lesson. The few words spoken by the teacher during this three-period lesson are shown in bold type in the following lesson outline:

Period 1. Teacher places the sandpaper letter *n* in front of the child. She traces the letter *n* with first two fingers then says, *'This is n.'* Repeats action and words three times.

Child traces *n* in manner demonstrated and says the sound *'n'*. Repeats three times.

Teacher traces the letter *d* then says *'This is d.'* Repeats action and words three times.

Child traces *d* in manner demonstrated and says the sound *'d'*. Repeats three times.

Period 2. Place both sandpaper letters for *n* and *d* in front of the child. Ask the child to *'Trace d. Point to n. Give me n.'*

Ask the child to perform five or more different actions.

Period 3. Teacher places one sandpaper letter in front of the child and asks

'What is this?'

She replaces the sandpaper letter with the second sandpaper letter and asks *'What is this?'*

The presenter had immediate feedback. There was no confusion in the child's mind because his full attention was on each letter presented to him along with the corresponding sound it represented according to a phonetic alphabet. The child heard and pronounced sounds clearly and knew how to trace letter shapes using the sandpaper letters. From this, he was able to make a connection between sounds in language and graphic writing. The ability to hear a sound and to recognize a letter was the basis for a Montessori child to be able to compose a word, a unit of meaning. If a child did not recognize a sandpaper letter in Period 3, he was invited to trace it with the first two fingers. His muscular memory (named the stereognostic sense by Montessori) helped the child to recall the sound associated with the letter because muscular memory is very strong at 4 years.

Listening for sounds in words

At the end of a three-period lesson with two sandpaper letters, Montessori continued by asking the child to listen as she spoke aloud some words beginning with the sound *n* (emphasising n). She then invited the child to think of and say words beginning with the sound *n*. Next she asked him to think of words with the sound *n* at the end and to articulate them. Finally, she asked for words with the sound *n* in the middle, and again the child was asked to pronounce the words precisely.

In Montessori's 1907 study, the 4-year-old child was helped to focus on listening for sounds in words and to become aware of their position in those words – at the beginning, at the end or in the middle. Children began this work using sandpaper letters at 3½ years or 4 years when Montessori found children to be in the appropriate sensitive period to learn to begin to write and read. They were able to hear sounds in words and identify letter shapes. She had discovered that children generally did not experience difficulty in hearing sounds in words. Their ears had been prepared to distinguish and pair sounds using different sensorial materials including sound boxes and bells. The final test for each child was to identify every sandpaper letter when blindfolded, by tracing the sandpaper letter with his first two fingers, using his stereognostic (muscular) sense and saying the sound it represented.

An opportunity to correct speech defects

Because each child perfected the mechanism of articular language between the ages of 2 and 7 years, 'in proportion as the hearing perceives better' (Montessori, 1964: 315), the pronunciation of the directress of the sound each letter represented had to be meticulously accurate. Montessori stressed that errors in articulate speech should be corrected early or they would persist into adulthood. Caring for the development of language at this formative stage for children eliminated the need for subsequent remedial work when children were older and the defects firmly established (ibid.: 325). Great importance was attached to the correction of speech defects as early as possible because she found that speech defects produced poor spellers, while children who pronounced words correctly were more successful spellers. It was further proof of that direct connection between spoken language and written language that Montessori had considered. She introduced directresses to the practice of correcting the defects in children's language (ibid.: 323) when introducing the sandpaper letters. A record was kept by the directress of each child's progress in pronunciation since it was 'a necessary part of learning graphic language' (ibid.: 280). A literate child needed to be able to speak clearly, pronouncing every word accurately. To Montessori, 'correct pronunciation is a necessary part of learning graphic language (ibid.: 279, 280). Her teachers were speech therapists.

Composing words using the movable alphabet

As soon as a child had been introduced to three or four sandpaper letters, he was introduced to the appropriately-named movable alphabet comprising ten copies of each alphabet letter, all in lower case. Vowels were in blue and consonants in red. The directress asked the child to select the letter from the movable alphabet to match the sound she said. When the child was able to select a few letters correctly and with confidence, he was encouraged to compose words. The time to introduce a child to composing words was 'left to the judgement of the teacher' (Montessori, 1964: 278) who had observed the child and knew his stage of development. If the child was unsuccessful in the lesson, the directress would know she had made an error of judgement. Montessori described in minute detail the direct teaching of a repeated syllable where both syllables had the same pronunciation with no stress on the second syllable. She discovered this herself when she trialled the materials. Her lesson plan is broadly as follows:

> The word 'mama' is pronounced very clearly stressing *m* in '*mama*'.
> The directress asks, 'What sounds can you hear in the word "*mama*"?'

The child replies 'm' and is invited to take the letter *m* from the alphabet tray.

The directress repeats '*ma – ma*'.

The child selects the letter *a* and places it beside the *m* making the syllable *ma*.

The child completes the second syllable without hesitation making *mama*.

Unique to Montessori schools, the movable alphabet helped children create or compose words by analysing them phonetically. Every word can be analysed according to its component sounds. Montessori found that it generally took about six weeks for 4-year-olds to compose words using the movable alphabet from the time they were first introduced to the sandpaper letters. She cited the Italian child who could compose any word pronounced clearly by the directress. 'He goes forward by himself composing his own words with signs corresponding to sounds, placing them one after the other,' she wrote (ibid.: 283).

Written language is super-natural

For all children, claimed Montessori, the natural function of spoken language involved a complex mechanism using small internal muscles which the child activated. Written language was essentially based on spoken language, but it was not a natural function of man because it 'adds itself to natural man' (ibid.: 317), making it 'super-natural', above nature and entirely man-made. Montessori saw writing as being a cultural, socially-constructed activity requiring 'new mechanisms' to be established permanently in the nervous system. They were far more simple than the movements required for a spoken word because the movements were 'performed by large muscles, all external, established by psycho-muscular mechanisms upon which we can directly act' (ibid.: 318). The hand needed to be prepared because children, she pointed out, were under 'immense strain when we set them to write directly without a previous motor education of the hand' (ibid.: 288).

Beginning handwriting

'Handwriting was quickly learned' Montessori stated, 'because we begin to teach only those who show a desire for it.' All the children in the first Casa were intensely interested in writing at 4 years of age, some at 3 ½ years. The average time between the first trials of the preparatory exercises (with the metal insets and sandpaper letters) to the child's first hand-written composed word (not dictated) for a child of 4 years was four to six weeks. For a child of 5 years, it was less than four weeks. Montessori observed and noted, 'Our children *handwrite well* from the moment in which they begin . . . it is surprisingly simple and is one of the easiest and most delightful of all conquests made by the child.' It was due to the fact that 'the minds and hands of our children are already *prepared* for writing' (Montessori, 1964: 294, 317). The hand of each 4 year old – using thumb, fore finger and middle finger-grip – was already prepared using sensorial materials, including knobbed cylinders, metal insets and sandpaper letters. Four-year-old children formed letters with ease. But, she observed, 6-year-old children experienced 'all sorts of depressing feelings' when they produced 'imperfect and erroneous signs' (ibid.: 294). They were bursting with keenness to write but struggled with the mechanics of writing. They were no longer attracted to or interested in working with the sandpaper letters, and they experienced more difficulty in coordinating their muscles. They would never be able to write letters as perfectly as they could have if training had started at 4 years (Montessori, 1964). These conclusions were the opposite of the advocates of the day who postponed the teaching of reading, and especially writing, till later rather than sooner.

'I can write! I can write!'

Montessori described in detail how she encouraged a boy in the first Children's House to write his first words. The child was prepared mechanically for writing having used the sandpaper letters and could compose words using a movable alphabet. She gave him chalk and asked him to draw a chimney and then encouraged him to write the word 'chimney'. On completion, the child called out excitedly. 'I can write! I can write! I know how to write!' Others crowded round to see, took up chalk and also began to write. It was the first time they had ever written, and they wrote whole words correctly (Montessori, 1964: 288). On that memorable day, they filled note books with words after they had experienced their first 'indescribable emotion of joy' at creating a written word (ibid.). The incident tellingly illustrates yet another of many 'mental explosions' described by Montessori and offers proof to her thesis that 'written language develops not gradually, but in an explosive way' (ibid.: 289). The achievement of children writing spontaneously at 4 years became headline news, worldwide.

Handwriting and the development of personality

As noted earlier in the chapter, children's hands were prepared for ventures in writing, after which they wrote 'entire words without lifting the pen' (Montessori, 1964: 295), while maintaining perfect slant, shape of letter and distance between each letter. Montessori tells us that a visitor once commented after observing a child at work: 'If I had not seen it I would not have believed it' (ibid.). She argued that there was 'educational value in this idea of preparing oneself before trying and of perfecting oneself before going on' (ibid.: 260) and claimed that it was a mistake for a child to continue 'to go forward boldly attempting things which he does imperfectly [because it] dulls the sensitivity of the child's spirit towards his own errors' (ibid.: 292). She had prepared children directly for handwriting at 4 years convinced that each child developed character traits which helped him perfect his personality. Handwriting contained 'an educative concept, teaching the child prudence to avoid errors, dignity to look ahead and guide him to perfection, and humility to make him strive to do better' (ibid.).

Dictation had its part in the writing skill. Montessori had the child write under dictation, which materially translates sounds into signs. For her, 'it was always easy and pleasant for a child to do, analogous to the development of the spoken language which is the motor translation of audible sounds' (ibid.: 267). Dictated writing was 'a perfect parallel with spoken language since a motor action must correspond with heard speech' (ibid.: 317). She saw much value in dictation because it was an opportunity to observe progress both in handwriting and in spelling. Note, that at any time, when a child needed to know a genre for some social function of writing, that child was given the help he needed to complete the task. A copy of a dictated letter written by a child of 5 years to Edwardo Tamalo was shown in the first edition of The Montessori Method (ibid.: 309).

In all of this work, Montessori had followed the child's natural stages in the development for spoken language – sounds, syllables, words and syntax. The emphasis she laid on children comprehending the direct link between speech and the written word was to help them become successful at composing and writing spoken words at 4 years of age. She had provided time for children to prepare their hands through sensorial materials, to use insets to learn pencil grip and control and to have sandpaper letters introduced by individual three-period lessons. Throughout, they traced sandpaper letters and perfected letter shapes through their stereognostic sense, they met and mastered the movable alphabet for composing words, phrases and sentences, and they acquired a phonemic awareness that enabled them to attack any new word they encountered in their subsequent lives. At 4 years, her children began to write words with confidence because of their knowledge of the link between sounds in language and letters of the alphabet. They had learned the processes for analysing words and for converting them to graphic language. The process was new, and it appeared to work for all children.

Montessori had observed in State Schools graphic language 'had always bristled with difficulties in its beginning because we have tried to make it perform the higher functions of the written language as soon as it has been acquired.' The higher functions of graphic language had taken civilization centuries to perfect. Montessori indicated that what was needed was 'a period of development of the higher functions which it was destined to perform later'. Mechanical written language would then have time to establish in the nervous system, become habit, independent of higher functions. By the time children had developed intellectually and were ready to use written language, mechanical written language was automatic (ibid.: 310–12). There is no desperate rush. The prepared child spontaneously 'explodes' into expressive writing on paper.

Beginning reading

Montessori designed a sequence of material and activities to help children learn to read with comprehension. The materials were designed so children could teach themselves. Their covert developmental language processes were all linked to the speech of each child who followed his own developmental programme and timetable. The Children's House was used as 'a field of scientific pedagogy', and Montessori's approach for learning to read was trialled, results confirmed and recorded in detail by Montessori. She described a child beginning to read:

> as one who has not heard the word pronounced, and recognises it when he sees it composed upon the table with the cardboard letters (movable alphabet) and can tell what it means. This child reads. So until the child reads a transmission of ideas from the written word, he does not read.
>
> (Montessori, 1964: 296)

In Montessori's view, spoken language was 'those little drops of sound [which] had wings' (ibid.: 316). Its counterpart was written language which translated sounds into signs – 'a motor translation of audible sounds' (ibid.: 266). She stressed that knowledge of the relationship between sounds and letters was sufficient for both beginning writing and beginning reading. She was convinced that once an Italian child read a word he had composed, his mind was prepared to say virtually every printed Italian word. That was a large claim, but it was reading Italian, mainly a phonetic language, at a mechanical stage only, being able to decode/encode, not focus on meaning.

Reading words was the beginning of reading

Montessori observed a child composing words and noted, 'Reading the word he had composed is not so easy' (Montessori, 1964: 283), because they could hear the sounds in a word when spoken by the directress but could not yet hear the sounds within a word he said to himself. Some 4–year-old children remained in this stage of development for a length of time before learning to listen for the sounds in words they said aloud. When they could do so, they exploded into reading words they had composed.

To see if a child was ready to read, Montessori made more trials. A word (noun) was composed by the directress in silence using a movable alphabet in front of the child. After a moment the child was asked: 'Bring this to me.' If successful the child progressed immediately to being presented with a longer word and was invited to bring that object. After several other trials with successful results, a card with one word was presented to the child which he had to interpret unaided and find the matching object. By presenting the child with one written word on a card 'we place the child before a new language', a graphic language which 'served to receive language transmitted to us by others' (ibid.: 301). If the child could interpret the word and find the matching object, that child could read.

Words were classified in boxes which 'helped develop schemata in each child's mind' (ibid.: 299). Because each child has to construct schemata himself, hundreds of reading cards were made by Montessori and her directresses in 1907, including the names of children, animals, flowers, insects, birds, cities, objects, colours, quantities and fruit. Each set of names was placed in a separate box. Children were observed reading every word in each box silently and when finished took another box of card to read. The directresses wrote more and more names but they could not satisfy the children's 'insatiable desire to read' (ibid.: 300). The activity was trialled again and duplicated successfully in Milan where the directress reported she had been writing cards for one-and-a-half hours and the children were 'not satisfied yet' (ibid.: 301). Every Montessori prepared environment contains words classified in boxes.

Word lovers

Between 4 and 7 years, 'children were word lovers and understood words' (Montessori, 1973b: 9). All activities used in 1907 for word reading survive intact today. Montessori found the children were greatly 'interested in reading out the alphabetic signs' all written on cards and 'their minds were working like adults who pore over pre-historic inscriptions' (ibid.: 36). They showed an interest in reading everything in their environment, some mothers reporting to her with delight that their offspring even read street names and shop signs. It became clear to Montessori 'that the children were interested not in reading the words but in puzzling out the alphabetic signs' (ibid.: 144). In that sense, reading became a problem-solving activity, an affair of the intelligence. Montessori allowed a period of time for children to puzzle out words. It was a mechanical ability which needed to be practiced so words could be read quickly and automatically. Children reading English required some extension materials, to help them master phonograms and rules, and so be able to write and read non-phonetic words. Montessori observed 'according to the type of individual, some write first and some read first' (Montessori, 1964: 266).

The Montessori approach to reading introduced in 1907 did away with primers for beginner readers. Children practised reading words mechanically before reading 'logical' text. She introduced these embryonic readers to many beautifully illustrated books given to her by friends and supporters. Directresses claimed that children read the books 'much more perfectly than children who had finished Second Elementary' (ibid.: 303). The 4–year-old children did read the words accurately but when they could not retell the stories, 'the complex thoughts of the writer had not been communicated to them and was to be one of the beautiful conquests of the future, a new source of surprise and joy' (ibid.: 301), she stopped the reading of books 'since they were not suited to our method' (ibid.) and waited for the time when children could understand what they had read without teacher intervention. A number of extra materials were needed for English, a non-phonetic language, before they could read with comprehension.

A discovery – composing and comprehending develop together

Montessori waited, observing the children during their period of inner preparation as they composed words with the movable alphabet, composed sentences with word cards and wrote words. She recorded how one day four children began writing sentences on the blackboard and 'their spontaneous compositions were a great surprise to me, and I was deeply moved' (Montessori, 1964: 304). These four children 'had arrived spontaneously at the art of composition just as they had spontaneously written their first word' (ibid.: 305) which prompted Montessori at that moment to write a question on the blackboard which the four children read slowly. They were silent for a moment then showed they understood and 'thus began between them and me a communication by means of written language, a thing which interested the children intensely because it transmits thought' (ibid.: 304). These four eager children read silently, understanding her meaning without a single spoken word because 'graphic language does not need spoken words' (ibid.: 305).

A silent reading experiment followed. Montessori wrote commands on red cards. The long sentences described actions which the children were to carry out. For example: Close the window blinds, open the front door, wait a moment and arrange things as they first were.

Children read these cards 'with intensity of attention . . . amid the most complex silence' (ibid.) and acted out the command exactly. Unexpectedly the command card game produced spontaneous discipline 'like some magic force, the magic of graphic language, the greatest conquest of civilization' (ibid.: 307). Command cards were the answer to the key problem of having children read aloud in schools to show they understood what they read. They were also an introduction to acting.

In Montessori education, writing precedes reading and composition precedes logical reading. Reading has to be mental not vocal in order for a child to receive an idea. Children are encouraged to read mentally to interpret thought. Written language must be isolated from articulate language when it comes to the interpretation of logical thought. It is language which 'transmits thought at a distance, while the senses and muscular mechanism are silent'. Written language 'is a spiritualised language which puts into communication all men who know how to read' (ibid.: 307).

Montessori and her directresses experimented to discover if children could read different fonts. The results were surprising; Montessori commented that 'in their mania for reading', the children to her amazement 'read not only the print, but the Gothic script on the calendar' (ibid.: 301). On the basis that children could read words in any font, she decided there 'remained nothing to do but the presentation of a book' (ibid.) stressing that 'the child who begins to read by interpreting thought should read mentally' (ibid.: 107). By reading silently, the child was able to attend to thinking about meaning and did not need to attend to the pronunciation of the words.

Reading was a silent activity

From the very start, in Montessori education, all reading activities were performed in silence. Observations of children had enabled Montessori to design materials to help them to read spontaneously with little intervention by the directress. Materials made it possible for children to discover, self-correct and teach themselves to begin to write, spell and read. The length of time for the process depended on each child's intelligence and interest in learning to read, along with the ability of the directress who intervened at the exact psychological moment. Children did not follow the programme in a linear fashion but took leaps forward using the materials they chose. The directress followed each child's path respecting the inner work of each child. Time was given for each child to master the complex processes of learning to read in his own way.

Oral reading

Montessori stressed that 'the child who begins to read by interpreting thought should read mentally' (Montessori, 1964: 307). By reading silently the child was able to attend to thinking about meaning and did not need to attend to the pronunciation of the words. At no time were children asked to read aloud a passage sight unseen because 'that was foreign to true reading and an impediment to the development of true reading'. It required the beginner reader to interpret the meaning *and* pronounce the words. It was far more difficult and complicated than speaking and reading perfectly, because it involved expressing someone else's thoughts using symbols. Interpretation was 'an affair of the intelligence while pronunciation was quite a different thing and secondary to interpretation' (Montessori, 1973b: 173–6).

Reading aloud in 1907 was the principal aspect of reading in State Schools. When Montessori had observed in these schools, she noted that the teacher had no reliable means of determining how much the child had understood and she never learned about her pupils' development because she continually interrupted to correct pronunciation, correct a word or assist by explanations and suggestions in interpretation (ibid.). The child spoke in a slow, monotonous voice as his eyes read words in a painful way and meaning was lost 'because meaning comes from the entire sentence' (ibid.: 172). While seeking meaning, a child's eyes traversed the sentence as a whole but his tongue could not keep up with pronunciation (ibid.: 173), and so the child was forced to stop to pronounce, or work out an unknown word, for his eyes and thoughts were moving more rapidly than his tongue could move. It was 'the eagerness of the child to learn that was cheated when he had to stop from working (thinking) because his tongue refused to act properly' (ibid.: 174). Reading aloud was a complex problem for all readers but especially for beginner readers since 'it is a combination of reading and expression. No wonder reading is one of the rocks on which the rudderless ship of elementary education inevitably runs aground' (ibid.: 176).

To Montessori, the function of oral reading 'was to bring immediate communication between two or more people which meant adding a kind of dramatic art to reading' (ibid.). From her observations and trials with new materials, she gathered psychological data to determine:

- what reading is, adapted to children at different stages of development
- the best ways of reading aloud
- the line of development followed by each child in that hidden mental world of his, cut off from our gaze.

(ibid.: 176–8)

Learning to read is a complex matter

Montessori observed that children read words silently first then written texts silently oral reading came later. These two processes were connected to articulate language and written language in a very complex covert manner. Montessori described her method and materials in great detail for language learning.

No research is available into silent reading for beginner readers at 4 years. This remains unique to Montessori education.

If at any stage a child wished or was asked to read aloud, the child chose a passage and practised it until he felt confident enough to read it aloud. To give a child a book and ask him to sight read brought much stress and anxiety to a child, and Montessori likened the experience to handing a speech with technical or medical terms throughout to be read by a person at random.

Luke and Gilbert (1993), Clay (1998), Burns et al. (1999) and Fields (2000) agree that learning to read is a long complex journey.

Mathematics

Montessori devoted ten pages to explain the materials for the introduction of counting in the Case dei Bambini. She used the materials she had trialled with deficient children and found that normal children 'very easily learn numeration which consists of counting objects' (Montessori, 1964: 326). She observed the many opportunities in daily life when children could count objects in their immediate environment. She introduced money so that children could learn to make change but suggested the use of good cardboard reproductions which she had seen used in London for their currency. There were three pieces of materials explained and illustrated for the introduction of zero to ten.

Materials consisted of:

1) Number rods – painted in red and blue divisions measuring 10 cm. from 1 to 10.
2) A Spindle box for correct amounts of spindles placed in compartments 0 to 9.
3) Small cubes and number cards marked 1 to 10 to be set out in an orderly manner.

There were sandpaper numerals in preparation for written examples and a brief explanation of how to use the number rods. Directresses were to collect small objects and make extension materials for addition, subtraction, multiplication and division (ibid.: 326–37).

There were so many opportunities to work with numbers in practical ways in daily life that it was left to the directress to use these for mathematics. For example the date, days of week, weeks in a month and year, date of birth, measuring own height, own weight, keeping records of own measurements, house number, telephone number are a very few numbers relevant to young children.

Note that by 1910, Montessori began devising materials for children aged 6 years to 12 years. Over a period of time some of these materials were brought down and introduced to the younger children. The Golden Beads allowed children at about 4 years to complete work for addition, subtraction, multiplication and division (without exchanging and then with exchanging) to 9999, after they fully understood the combinations of numbers to 10. Materials were also introduced at 4 years for algebra (binomial and trinomial cubes) and all geometric plane figures in a geometric cabinet.

All the practices and discoveries made in the first Casa dei Bambini during 1907 and 1908 were the basis for all future experiments in Montessori education.

Critics and supporters from 1907

There have always been critics and supporters of Montessori education from the start. Reports of children's successes in the first Casa dei Bambini (1907) were reported in the *London Times* and in newspapers and magazines in the United States. Educators travelled to Rome to meet Montessori and visit the Casa dei Bambini. Reports were mixed.

In the United States, as early as 1912, Elizabeth Rose Shaw denounced Montessori education in an article in the *National*

Educational Association journal (Willcott, 1968). William Heard Kilpatrick, a colleague of John Dewey, returned to the United States after spending a year in Rome observing Montessori's work. He was her chief critic and discredited her work in his book *Montessori System Examined*, published in 1914, claiming that 'Montessori had nothing new' and the Method represented theory more than half a century behind the times (Kilpatrick, 1914: 63). Within a few years his book and comments effectively stopped academics' interest in the Montessori Method in the United States (Lillard, 1972; Kramer, 1976; Phillips, 1979; Potts, 1980). Kilpatrick (1914) noted that 'to teach the 3Rs before eight years was at best a waste of time, and might possibly be harmful'. The criticisms in the United States were so effective that Montessori lost many of her supporters.

Dorothy Canfield Fisher, an American psychologist and a writer (better known for her novels), spent the winter months of 1911 and 1912 with Montessori and attended her first teacher training sessions in Rome. She had read the Italian edition of *The Montessori Method* and found herself 'ignorant of medical facts about physiological psychology and the nervous system of the human being' (Fisher 1913: 16, 17). She had been converted to Montessori education, declaring that Montessori had 'a purely medical interest in children's brains . . . and had discovered certain laws about the intellectual activities of childhood in general' (ibid.: 17). Fisher tended to agree with Kilpatrick that in essence the confirmed scientific proofs Montessori found actually 'had nothing new, nothing that we do not admit in theory, although we do not have the courage to act on them' (ibid.: 18). But then, Montessori did not begin with a theory. She acted on what children revealed to her through observation. Also, she had never claimed to have invented anything new, as Evans reported in 1971. In Montessori's own words, 'Had I wished to pass as an inventor, I would have been shown up' (Potts, 1980: 37). Moreover, she acknowledged many sources through her writings.

Years later at a course in India, sometime between 1939 and 1944, Montessori recalled that Charlotte Bühler, in Vienna (about 1914), was 'an authoritative exponent of experimental psychology and had reached the conclusion that the mental faculties of children under five years of age are impermeable to any form of culture'. This, 'in the name of science', was like 'a kind of tombstone placed over our experiments' (Montessori, 1975: 22).

A. M. Joosten attended some of Montessori's last courses given in India (between 1939 and 1944). He defended Montessori, noting that 'she had applied her genius and scientific knowledge to the penetration and application of her discovery'. That, he explained, is why 'she ever and most energetically disclaimed to have invented a method of education which was a statement of fact'. He went further, declaring that what she did above all else 'was to shake the conscience of the world towards the unexplored and neglected wealth hidden in human nature' (Joosten, 1955: 4, 5). The great difference between Montessori education and most other systems of education was that it was based on the development of the child, and therefore, followed the laws of nature.

Beryl Edmonds challenged Montessori's claim that the children taught themselves, arguing 'that by showing a child how to use materials the teacher is imposing the method and is "teaching him"' (Edmonds, 1976: 4).

Shelley Phillips commented that 'Montessori was enormously afraid that her theories would be misapplied but she did not worry about sampling, control of variables or statistical checks' (Phillips, 1979: 63).

Since the 1970s, hundreds of researchers have studied children's reading and searched for the best teaching methods. Thousands of reading samples have been recorded and analysed later. Millions of words have been written on this topic.

In 1980, Brian Cambourne and Peter Rousch claim that 'researchers were looking for the best way to teach reading but teachers ignored what was going on in children's heads, paying little attention to the processes used by children'. There was no technology for 'getting inside readers heads and under the scalp into brain tissues' but the best way to observe intellectual processes in action was 'to analyse errors as children read print'. By observing children guessing, sounding out and working out words 'reveals what goes on in the head'. Specially trained analysts, 'gained a complete picture of mental processes, a window to the mind' (Cambourne and Rousch, 1980: 107–8). This was a big claim. There were researchers who analysed every error (12,000 errors from 20 different perspectives) and found surprising results including 'reading is not an exact process with good readers making the same number of errors as poor readers' when reading out loud. Seventy per cent of readers did not attempt to correct errors. Proficient readers 'get back on track if meaning is lost', but low ability readers 'tolerate semantic nonsense' (ibid.: 110, 111).

More recent brain research with scanners which can get under the scalp and into brain tissues has discovered what triggers thought in the area of the brain which deals with language, but still researchers have not been able to discover what and how the mind works, and perhaps never will (Schiller, 2000).

Implications for education

Much of education has continued to be based on theory rather than on the study of the child, that is *nature* and the laws of nature. Montessori always based her work on the study and observations of each child and not on theories, which she considered to be 'opinions and not truth' (Montessori Course, London, 1946). However, Naturalistic Inquiry has attracted psychologists since the 1980s, including Jerome Harste, an educator. To him, naturalistic research is theory building rather than theory building methodology, and ethnography is inductive, meaning that observation is developed into a theory or explanation of observations. The type of research

Montessori conducted could be known today as 'naturalistic research', and her book *The Montessori Method* in which she reported her first experiments at the Casa dei Bambini as an ethnography. 'Naturalistic education' is not new, and according to Ornstein some of the most outstanding educational philosophers are linked with it, including 'Comenius, Rousseau, Pestalozzi, Owen and Spencer' (Ornstein, 1977: 117).

Today, observation of children is a respected method for classroom research.

Relation to current issues and research

Direct or indirect teaching of sound/s in language

The study of linguistics today includes meta-linguistics, the analysis of speech and language in terms of its structure (sentences, words, phonemes, syntax and pragmatics). These orientations require the individual to be able to view language and speech as an object when everyday use of language is used for communication, centred around meanings and not structure. Essentially, children beginning writing or reading must have 'word awareness' (a word is a unit of speech) and 'phonemic awareness' (to segment words into phonemic elements) (Galbraith, 1991). Much research began in the 1970s and a few are listed below.

Chomsky (1971) and Read (1975) agreed that some children could analyse words but Downing and Oliver (1973–4: 568–82) found in their research that 'many children do not have a well constructed concept of a word'.

Bissex (1980: 13, 119) describes how she asked children, 'What sounds are in *mumps*?' She stressed that when children are 'making passage from language heard to language seen, sound awareness is a key concept'.

Bradley and Bryant (1983), Lundberg (1984), Tunmer et al. (1984) and Henderson (1984) all emphasize the need for children to develop 'meta-linguistic' orientation to speech and language.

Hall (1987: 60) noted that Downing observed that many children, 3 to 7 years, fail to distinguish sounds and letters and 'are cognitively confused'.

Lungberg (1984) saw that it was necessary to deliberately draw each child's attention to 'a word' and to the 'phonemic properties' of speech and sometimes this was more effectively done if 'drawn out of context, beyond meaning'. Research findings indicate that these particular skills do indeed require explicit teaching.

Several researchers suggest that training young children in rhyme and alliteration helps the development of phonemic awareness, but Galbraith (1991: 15, 16) emphasizes that 'it is not sufficient for phonemic awareness skills to be embedded in a rhyming story on the hope that the child will somehow "pick up" phonemic awareness'. She prefers direct teaching.

Yopp and Singer (1994: 382) point out that Kindergarten children are not consciously aware of words in sentences or that 'words can be segmented into phonemes'. The article discusses how children, they were observing in the United States, after one year at school (6 to 7 years of age) are asked to hear a sound in the middle, the beginning and the end of a word. The teachers see this 'as being essential for reading progress'.

Ong (in Street, 1995: 154) spoke of the 'vocalic alphabet' which was 'a breakthrough, representing sound graphically' and that writing was 'representation of sounds'.

Williams (1995) (in Clay, 1998: 56) points out that 'phonemic awareness is about awareness of sounds in speech (phonemes) within the speech stream' while 'listening involves how to listen and what to listen for'.

Kale and Luke (in Riordan, 1997: 116) point out that there is a broad consensus among linguists and psychologists that 'children need to learn how to manipulate language to facilitate the development of more complex cognitive processes'.

Clay (1998: 51, 73) made observations which showed 'that recognition of letters evolves slowly in young children because they are trying to hear phonemes and at the same time to distinguish between letters that look the same to him'. She claimed that many children are confused.

In Montessori education, each child at 3 years of age became aware of the sounds in language when he was introduced to the sandpaper letters during a three-period lesson and at the same time prepared himself, physically and psychologically, to write every letter of the alphabet on his own. There was no confusion.

Beginning readers

Schonell, whose work on beginning reading was based on scientific, psychological research, once noted that 'beginner readers with young, immature minds need opportunities and time "to sort things out", to understand what they are doing' (Schonell, 1945: 6).

Holdaway pointed out that 'since the pioneering work of McKinnon (1959) there has been a wealth of research indicating that children find great satisfaction in puzzling out the problems of interpreting print' (Holdaway, 1979: 210).

Working out puzzles and codes brings great satisfaction to children and adults alike.

Speech training

One of Montessori's outstanding students in regard with speech training was Dr Anne McAllister, who became a leading authority in speech training at Jordanhill Teachers' College, Glasgow, and whose books and methods were found in most English-speaking Teacher-Training Colleges throughout the world in the 1950s and

1960s. Today, the Department of Speech Therapy at the University of Strathclyde, Jordanhill Campus, is a leader of Speech Therapy in the United Kingdom (Strathclyde People, 1999). Teachers are no longer trained to teach speech training in classrooms and refer pupils-in-need to a speech therapist or advise parents to take action.

Teacher Training and the Early Dissemination of Montessori Education

3

Teacher training

In 1907, when Montessori was able to repeat the successful results enjoyed in the first Casa dei Bambini by providing exactly the same learning conditions for children in the second Casa, she realized the need to train teachers because she could not be everywhere to ensure the correct conditions were being provided. A third Casa was opened in Milan on 18 October 1907 and a fourth in Rome on 4 November 1907. Plans were also set in train to convert all Italian-Swiss orphanages into Children's Houses in January 1909, so the first training course was planned. The preliminary results derived from the experiments in the first Casa were to provide the basis of all future teacher-training programmes, and over the years Montessori continued to study children from birth to 18 years.

The first Montessori teacher training course

The first teacher training course away from a Casa dei Bambini in Rome was held in 1909 at the villa La Montesca, home of Barone and Baroness Franchetti near Citta di Castello. One hundred students attended. The course comprised of lectures on:

- Montessori's educational philosophy
- teachers as observers (researchers) of free children as individuals
- the classroom (a prepared environment) was a laboratory
- principles of Scientific Pedagogy with individual children as case studies
- demonstrations of how children taught themselves (local children used)
- spontaneous self development of the individual
- establishment of scientific child psychology
- demonstrations by Montessori with local children in how to put her method into practice including presentations of Three Period Lessons.

(Kramer, 1976: 136–8)

Montessori's methodologies were radically new, not different revamps of the old practices that required teachers to fill in the gaps of theories. She introduced an entirely new, carefully prepared learning environment in which the child took centre-stage. Those attending this first course had opportunities to observe the local children working freely as independent individuals in what was already a typical Montessori classroom. She demonstrated how children taught themselves and the student-teachers witnessed for themselves the spontaneous self-development of the individual. Most important of all, they observed and practised the psychology Montessori was promoting based on allowing children to take charge of their own work schedules and engage in self-instruction without interruption from the teacher at all. It was a dramatic break from the past where teachers of the old school were immersed in theory. Attendees had to relearn when to intervene and to understand that their task was passive, their role being to observe and understand without interfering in whatever the child was doing (Montessori, 1964: 87). They also had to refrain from offering needless help which was 'a hindrance to the development of natural forces' (ibid.: 226) and to desist from talking too much instead of quietly observing. Montessori expressed a preference for untrained, inexperienced teachers on the grounds as it was easier for them to put her principles into action without the built-in biases of trained teachers.

After the success of this course in 1909, Baroness Franchetti persuaded Montessori to compile her qualitative research findings and to write them up for other teachers to share. She stayed on at the villa and within three weeks her work was completed under the heading *Il Metodo della Pedagogia Scientifica applicator all'educazione nelle Case dei Bambini (1909) / Scientific Pedagogy as Applied to Children's Education in the Children's Houses 1909.*

Published in 20 languages in 1912, and as *The Montessori Method* in English, it described in detail what Montessori had discovered in the first *Case dei Bambini* (Children's Houses). It sold out in four days and still remains a best seller. Its simple message was that *understanding the development of a child was the key to education.* Montessori had conducted a scientific study of each child to explain child development between the ages of 2½ years and 6 years within the Children's House.

Preparation of a new directress/researcher

The classroom as a laboratory was a very new idea in 1907. In essence, Montessori education became a Scientific Pedagogy, put into practice that year by Montessori and her teachers. Montessori noted that teachers of the old school were prepared in principles of philosophy, so immersed in theory that 'they remained forever in the field of theory . . . left standing without the door of real experimental science and that experience which makes real scientists'. The new directress was to become a researcher who needed to be 'a worshipper of nature' possessing a self-sacrificing spirit of a scientist and a reverent love for the child from whom she would 'learn how to perfect herself as an educator' (Montessori, 1964: 8–13). For Montessori, intelligent teachers training to become directresses 'understood the principles of the method but had great difficulty putting it into practice' (ibid.: 87). Those difficulties included: knowing when to intervene, understanding the principle that children teach themselves, converting to child-centred education, leaving as much as possible to nature so they could observe and not offer needless help (ibid.: 87–226).

Nearly 70 years later, Stenhouse (1975) proposed the idea of the teacher as researcher. He pointed out:

> Educational ideas expressed in books are not easily taken into possession by teachers . . . (yet) curricular specifications expose them to testing by teachers . . . the idea is that in educational science, in which each classroom becomes a laboratory, each teacher is a member of the scientific community.
>
> (Stenhouse, 1975: 142)

Critics and supporters

Switzerland (1909)

Among the very first nations to manifest interest was Switzerland, largely through the endeavours of Teresina Bontempi (1883–1968) and the University of Geneva. Bontempi had closely followed Montessori's first course in 1909, and within two years, established a number of Children's Houses in Switzerland. The University of Geneva, already with an international reputation at the cutting edge of contemporary educational practices, invited Montessori to demonstrate her method in person with a group of young children (3-6 years) at its Jean-Jacques Rousseau Institute, in the presence of three of its teaching staff – Professors Pierre Bovet (1878–1965),

Edouard Claparede (1873–1940) and Adolphe Ferriere (1879–1960). At that demonstration Jean Piaget (1896–1980) first came in contact with Montessori's educational innovations (Association Montessori: Suisse www.montessori-ams.ch). He was deeply impressed and was the start of his distinguished career in education. Out of his own detailed observations emerged his ideas of cognitive development. It is worth noting here that Piaget took part in the Second International Montessori Congress in Nice (1931) and in the fourth one in Rome (1934) where he presented a paper titled 'On the development of the geometric thought of the child'. Pierre Bovet also took part in that Congress. In 1932, Montessori visited Switzerland, including in her lectures tour of Geneva, Lausanne, Berne, Zurich and Bellinzone. Her book *Education and Peace* (1972) appeared in Geneva at that time, along with the birth of the Swiss Montessori Society with Piaget as its first President and Elisabeth Rotten, the celebrated pacifist, as first Vice-President. She became President of AMI in 1939 (Association Montessori Internationale, 2005: 1–3). Montessori noted in 1909 that all Swiss Kindergartens were to become Montessori environments in 1910, and by 1911 Montessori education was introduced into Swiss schools (Müller and Schneider, 2002).

Teacher training in Rome from 1910

Because of the great demand for teacher training, Montessori gave up everything else to do all teacher training herself. Two teacher training courses were planned for 1910 in Rome (Kramer, 1976: 145). The first in Italian and the second in English because of the interest shown in her method from the United States of America and England. They were held at the Franciscan convent on Va Diusta in Rome.

Dorothy Canfield Fisher, a novelist from the United States, with an interest in education, spent the winter months of 1911 and 1912 with Montessori and attended her teacher training sessions in Rome. In her book published in 1913, Fisher gives a clear insight into

Montessori education and the content of the first teacher training course. To her, much of what Montessori observed was rediscovered facts and one was 'the old threadbare truism that every child is different from every other child. We all knew this and disregarded it while Montessori took it fully into account.' By considering the psychological aspects of each child, '"class recitation" (rote learning) and "class lessons" were out of the question' (Fisher, 1913: 19). Montessori was able to show that class lessons could possibly fit the needs of one child, but it was possible the class lesson did not in fact fit the needs of any child in the class, and so 'things must somehow be organised and arranged, that for most of the time, the child can and shall teach himself' and the *less intervention*, the more quickly and spontaneously he would learn (ibid.: 19, 20).

By 1913, the Montessori method was being put into practice in infant schools in Italy, Switzerland, France, England, Argentina, America and Australia. That same year, the Montessori Education Society was set up in the United States and the National Montessori Committee in London. Both were the forerunners of world bodies that have kept alive the movement begun with the first Casa dei Bambini.

That same year when Montessori organized the international training course in Rome participants flocked to attend, not only from the host country, Italy and other European countries, but also from further afield including South Africa, Australia, India, China, the Philippines and the United States.

In one of those lectures, Montessori elaborated on her idea of the child's natural psychic development based on the immutable laws of nature:

> The very young child begins to walk; he feels an irresistible impulse which impels him to do so. We could not hold back the child from walking, and if we did, it would be a form of violence and would have serious effects on his motor development. The child begins to speak because his development leads him to do so. The child does not develop because he wishes to utilize these developments.
>
> (Chattin-McNichols, 1991: 45)

It was what she perceived as a general principle underlying all development during the whole of childhood, not just during infancy. In that same lecture she spelled out what it was that she saw as a weakness in the traditional state system:

> One of the errors of the established method of education is that it only takes into consideration the utilization of the things which are developed. For instance, it is considered useless to develop writing in the child before the child is able to utilize this accomplishment, and it seems only necessary to develop when he is able to use it. When, in my method of education, I lay down this principle of development in itself as the fundamental basis of all, an objection was raised that there would be difficulty in making the social application of these things which have been developed, because man must develop these capacities for utilization.
>
> (Ibid.: 46)

In Montessori classrooms all children were exposed to enriching stimuli, and each child was allowed to make his own choice. Those who were ready to make the leap into reading and writing, were perfectly free to make that huge step rather than waiting until the system decided they were of the correct chronological age to do so.

Dissemination of Montessori education

One of the greatest difficulties Montessori faced was how to encourage new teachers to put her principles into practice, to follow her experiment and to procure the same results. She decided to do all teacher training herself which meant she had to travel extensively giving lectures, speaking at conferences, writing articles and books while conducting teacher training courses on four continents. Several Australians and New Zealanders attended her courses in Italy and other European centres.

There were reports of several countries opening Montessori schools and everywhere there was a desperate need for teacher training. There were many supporters of the Montessori method and Montessori Societies were established on every continent. Many schools were established by teachers who had read *The Montessori Method* or had attended Montessori lectures and courses. Although Montessori constantly went on lecture tours, the centre of activity was in Rome where she conducted many international courses.

Presentations of materials

In all her training courses, Montessori fully explained her didactic materials and how precisely she expected them to be demonstrated.

The three-period lesson

A three-period lesson was used for the introduction of the rough and smooth boards and the colour tablets only as the other practical life and sensorial materials were demonstrated in silence. But the lesson was used countless times each day to name and introduce the language which described the qualities of each piece of material and to introduce the sandpaper letters. Each lesson was given to each child individually (Montessori, 1964: 45). The characteristics of the three-period lessons used by Montessori were:

brevity (teacher used few words)
simplicity (spoke only the truth)
objectivity (child concentrated on the materials being demonstrated).

The three-period lesson had to be seen by the presenter as 'an explanation of the object and of the use the child can make of it'. The aim was that the attention of the child was to concentrate on the object and not the teacher's personality. All lessons were based on Itard's experiments so 'each lesson corresponds to an experiment' (Montessori, 1964: 108, 109). Each lesson was short and some lasted less than 1 minute.

Montessori commented that teachers attending her courses 'are greatly surprised at such simplicity' declaring 'everybody knows how to do that! . . . but the truth is that not everyone knows how to do this simple thing, to give a lesson with such simplicity . . . to conform to the standards of clearness, brevity and truth, is particularly a very difficult matter' (ibid.: 110). The three-period lesson proved to be one of the most difficult things for trained teachers to perfect. If the teacher made a mistake in her demonstration, the child repeated the mistake because he repeated every action exactly, even those which were wrong. It was essential for the directress to demonstrate precisely and not confuse the child. At the end of the lesson the child was told he may choose that material at any time. If at any time during the three hour work cycle a child wished to be introduced to some piece of material, he could ask for a lesson. The directress introduced the material, the child worked with it and did the learning. Montessori's motto was to explain anything as briefly as possible.

Montessori changed the name of teacher to directress who was responsible to direct each young child into 'the world of human thought' (ibid.: 237) simply by introducing the child to the didactic materials and not through talk. After a child became familiar with the piece of material, he began to experiment, to make discoveries and take shortcuts which were a sign of intelligence. Montessori claimed that children taught themselves. Teachers had to put their trust in both the materials and the child.

Europe

Criticism of Montessori's work began as early as 1909 after the publication of *Il Metodo* when psychologists challenged Montessori's spectacular results in reading and writing with young children aged 4 years. Montessori responded tartly that such critics appeared to question 'if the mental life of the child ought not to be immolated in favour of useless results because a little later on, a child over six years can learn to read and write'. (Montessori, 1975: 22). In Germany, in 1914, Charlotte Bühler, an authoritative exponent of experimental psychology, reached the conclusion that the mental faculties of children under 5 years of age were 'impermeable to any form of culture'. For Montessori, such an assertion in the name of science 'was like a tombstone placed over our experience' (ibid.), the failure of official education to attain similar results an indictment of their methods. By 1939, 30 years later, Montessori noted that psychologists 'were starting to concentrate on the development of very young children from the earliest stage' and among them was Charlotte Bühler (Montessori, 1967a: 4).

From 1914, Berlin became the heartland of Montessori education in Europe as the consequence of the work of Hilde Hecker, Elsa Ochs and Elizabeth Achwartz, all of whom had attended Montessori's second international course in Rome that year. They were later supported by the educator Clara Grunwald. Both Ochs and Grunwald were ardent supporters of Montessori education and joined the Association of Resolute Schools Reformers in Berlin where the principles of Montessori Method were discussed. In 1919, Grunwald established the German Montessori Committee which quickly set up Children's Houses for children of working-class families. Three years later the Society of Friends and sponsors of the Montessori Movement were also established in Germany. In 1925 the two bodies merged to form the German Montessori Society with Grundwald as its head. Montessori herself boosted the fledging movement in Germany with visits in 1922, 1925, 1926, 1927. But the shortage of funds in post-World War I Germany, still struggling from crippling debt, along with a conservative reluctance to move too far from Fröebelian principles and a dearth of trained Montessori teachers, militated against wider acceptance. By 1923, the demand for Montessori education outstripped the capacity of the limited number of teachers to satisfy the need, and Elsa and Clara ran the first teacher-training course in Germany. By 1927, differences between Montessori and Grundwald over the latter's organizing of her own training workshop flared up and a faction formed within the Berlin group. Montessori refused to sign the certificates of those who had attended Grundwald's training courses. When another body, the German Association of Montessori Education, formed in 1929, Montessori took over the presidency and Grundwald was denied membership. That year, Montessori had established the Association Montessori Internationale (AMI) with headquarters in Berlin. When the Nazis came to power in 1933, all schools run by the national body headed by Montessori in Berlin, Breslau, Guben, Jena, Leipzig, Cologne, Aachen and Freiberg were closed with others run by Grunwald and private children's Houses (Müller and Schneider, 2002: 37). By 1936, the Montessori movement in Germany was 'crushed' (ibid.: 53). All Montessori schools in German-occupied countries were closed. It was not until 1947 when Irene Dietrich was able to open a Montessori class in the British sector of Berlin, and soon after Montessori education was practised in secondary school (ibid.: 139).

Individuals and organizations have promoted Montessori education in Europe since 1909. In 1920, Montessori spoke of her fundamental ideas of secondary education at the University of Amsterdam and by 1930 the first Lyceum (grammar school) had opened. In 2000, The Montessori College Oost, designed by Herman Hertzberger, a former Montessori pupil, 'is the first building in the world to have been especially built as a Montessori secondary school' (Müller and Schneider, 2002: 139). The 1,600 multinational students enrolled are aged 12 to 18 years. In the Netherlands and Belgium students have the option of attending a state school or a Montessori school because Montessori education is officially recognized by their Departments of Education.

As in many countries, it was women who introduced the Montessori system into Denmark, the first Dane being Marie Helms in 1911 with 'a charming and comprehensive article on Montessori's Kindergartens in Rome' (Nasgaard, 1929: 61). Thora Constintin-Hansen read this article and began to convert two of the classes in the school for crippled children, 8–10 years of age, into Montessori classes. According to Constintin-Hansen, the invalid children became 'quieter and better balanced, and sank themselves into their work'. She proposed the whole school of 100 children be converted to Montessori but met with opposition from the Committee of the Crippled Children's House, so Montessori's practices could not be trialled there. In 1917, she helped to found the Montessori Society in Denmark and with two colleagues the following year opened the Danish Montessori Society's School at Frederikssund in a quiet, remote villa looking out over the Roskilde Fjord. There 'the most radical educational reforms in Denmark were carried out'. Soon she helped establish other Montessori classes throughout Denmark. There are other champions of the Montessori movement mentioned in this article including Erik Erikson, a devoted supporter of Montessori education in Denmark and several places in Europe before sailing to the United States.

Montessori's first visit to the United States in 1913 – supporters and critics (see Chapter 2)

Montessori's success was well known in the United States before World War I (Phillips, 1979: 57; Kramer, 1976: 375). Willcott (1968: 49) noted that 'in 1911, a frenzy took place in education' over articles published about Montessori's work, and by 1912, 65 Americans, including University lectures from Harvard and Yale, travelled to Rome to study under Montessori; 'so many travelled to Rome'. *The Montessori Method* was published in English in 1912 and criticized by C. E. Morgan as having 'a lack of cultivation and analysis of higher thought processes and feeling' (Potts, 1980: 41). On her first visit to the United States in 1913, Montessori was invited to the White House and gave a public lecture at Carnegie Hall where more than a thousand people were turned away (Kramer, 1976). She lectured in Italian to a full house and John Dewey presided (Willcott, 1968: 49). A group of influential people had formed a Montessori Association including Alexander Graham Bell as president and Margaret Wilson (daughter of US President Wilson) as Hon. Secretary (Phillips, 1979: 57).

Enthusiasm in the United States was short-lived because of critics. Elizabeth Ross Shaw in an article in the national Educational Association Journal in 1912 (Willcott, 1968: 50) denounced Montessori because she taught children to read and write before 6 years. William heard Kilpatrick, a colleague of John Dewey, returned to the United States after spending months in Rome observing Montessori education. He too discredited Montessori in his book *Montessori System Examined* (1914) claiming. Montessori had nothing new. It is ironic that in 1925, Kilpatrick 'argued for more individualized curricula and expressed dissatisfaction with whole class instruction' (Good, 1983: 1).

Montessori visited the United States again in 1915 for the World Fair held in San Francisco. A huge attraction was the Montessori classroom viewed by thousands of visitors through glass walls. The class directress was Helen Parkhurst who was later to help develop the Dalton Plan for disadvantaged children experiencing difficulties in learning to read. During this visit Montessori conducted a Montessori Training Course in California. A Montessori school had been established in the home of Alexander Graham Bell (Lillard, 1972: 8). The following year, 1916, Edmonson reported there were 189 authorized Montessori schools and 2,000 unauthorized schools in the United States. Continued attacks on Montessori by Frances Wayland Parker and William Heard Kilpatrick outweighed the influence on Montessori in academic circles in the United States, and by the 1920s 'reference to Montessori in the academic community was infrequent' (Edmonson, 1963: 67). Thirty years later, two years after World War II, Montessori presented a paper on 'Education and Peace' to UNESCO in 1947.

The decline of Montessori education in the United States lasted for more than 50 years. It was not until a decade after World War

II, when Nancy McCormack Rambusch reintroduced Montessori to United States in 1957 after completing a course at St Nicholas in London, that a second phase of interest began for Montessori Education. Montessori teacher training courses flourish in the United States today.

Individuals promoting Montessori since then have established organizations to satisfy the need for Montessori teachers. In 1971, Helen K. Billings established the Montessori Institute of America (MIA) based in Kansas City, MO, and soon afterwards Tim Seldin, with long experience running a Montessori school in Silver Spring, MD, became President of the Montessori Foundation and Chairman of the International Montessori Council (IMC). Lee Havis began the National Center for Montessori Education (NCME) which in 1979 became the International Montessori Association (IMA). Another meriting mention is David Kahn, executive director of the North American Montessori Teachers' Association and founding programme director of Hershey Montessori Farm School which follows Montessori's *Erdkinder* principles at its campus at Huntsberg, OH.

Turbulent years – World War I

It is impossible to measure the full impact World War I (1914–18) had on the Montessori educational movement, but Montessori saw the beginning of a decline in the popularity of her theories and practices. She continued to travel to the Americas in 1915. In 1916 her third book *L'autoeducazione nell Scuole Elementri* was published (in two volumes) which described the application of her system to primary children. That year she conducted her fourth international training course for teachers in Rome. She resigned her professorship at the University of Rome and at the invitation of the Barcelona City Fathers moved her home and base there. In 1917 there were lectures in New York and the Netherlands where a Montessori Society was founded. 1918 saw the end of World War I and the opening of 20

Montessori schools in Naples. That year Montessori was received in a private audience by Pope Benedict XV.

The following year, 1919, Montessori oversaw the establishment of the first German Montessori Committee in Berlin and embarked on a lecturing programme at Amsterdam University and in Paris, Milan and Rome. It was in Amsterdam that Montessori first brought to public attention her ideas on secondary school education. A committee of academics from all universities in Holland was set up to examine the application of her method in the teaching of history, geography and science to high school students. Hitherto, the Montessori Method had been applied exclusively to infants and primary students.

Italy

Rome was the centre of Montessori education and teacher training, but when Mussolini 'marched on Rome in 1922' (Kneller, 1951), Montessori took up residence in Barcelona with her son Mario, but she continued to travel to Italy constantly. Her last visit was in 1934 (Lillard, 1972: 15). At the outbreak of the Spanish Civil War in 1936, Montessori and Mario 'fled to England' (Cohen, 1974: 62), and 'she continued to visit Italy from there until 1938' (Kramer, 1976). When Mussolini joined Hitler, all Montessori schools were closed in Italy and throughout all occupied countries during World War II. However, Montessori did return to Rome soon after the war in 1945 to conduct her first teacher training course for children from birth to 3 years. The history of Montessori education in Italy is sparse, but several articles document how Montessori spread Montessori education herself. The writings of Kneller (1951), Standing (1957), Edmonson (1963), Lillard (1972), Cohen (1974), Kramer (1976), Berryman (1980) and Sullivan (1985) give a documented account. All help to sketch a picture of what happened to Montessori and Montessori education. Today many students from every part of the globe travel to Bergamo,

Italy, to attend Montessori courses for children from birth to 12 years conducted by Association Internationale (AMI) whose President is Renilde Montessori, granddaughter of Maria Montessori.

Montessori in Australia

Montessori did not visit Australia but as early as 1909 her name was known to Peter Board, Director of Education in New South Wales through reports in the *London Times*. When *The Montessori Method* was published in English in 1912, a copy was obtained by Peter Board and made available to Miss Margaret Simpson, Infant Mistress at Blackfriars School in Sydney where she was in charge of teacher training in New South Wales. Miss Simpson was selected to travel to Italy to study under Montessori at the first teacher training course held in Rome in 1913 (Crane and Walker, 1957; Petersen, 1971; O'Donnell, 1996). In 1922, Peter Board retired from the New South Wales Education Department at the time when children up to 9 years of age were receiving Montessori education in some State Schools (Turney, 1972). The new Director of Education introduced 'new' theories and methods. By the 1930s there was little of Montessori education to be found in State Schools. Montessori education was left to a few privately run Children's houses. There are some parallels to be found between what happened in the United States and in Australia. Montessori education faded during the 1930s (ibid.).

After World War II there were a number of European migrants arriving in Australia who had attended Montessori schools and some had done teacher training. Mrs Duyker de Vries from Holland studied under Montessori in 1939 and opened a school in Perth, Western Australia for children 3 years to 6 years. Over the years her school grew and catered for students to 18 years. Her school has survived and those choosing academic work present themselves for the International Baccalaureate.

Montessori in the British Isles

It was 1919 before Montessori reached England to conduct her first teacher training course in London. By then there were several Montessori schools for children till 12 years of age started by teachers who had attended teacher training courses in Rome. The proposed teacher training course had 2,000 applications of which 250 were selected. The two-month course began on 1 September 1919 at St Bride's Foundation in Fleet Street, London. Lily Hutchinson, who had attended the 1913 course in Rome, acted as interpreter. The two-month course consisted of

- 50 hours of lectures for children 3 years–11 years by Montessori
- 50 hours of teaching practice
- 50 hours of observation in recognized Montessori classrooms
- 3 evening meetings per week for debate and discussion
- every student prepared a manual with drawings and lessons for every piece of material
- written and oral examinations.

On completion, a diploma to teach, signed by Montessori, was granted but not to teacher train. The fee was 35 Guineas, or 20 Guineas for those who already held the Infant Course Diploma (Kramer, 1976: 305).

The same format was kept for all Montessori courses. There were lectures, demonstrations, practice teaching, a manual, a book of materials to be made followed by written and oral examinations, although the courses varied in length. The format remains today with some minor alterations depending which teacher training course is selected.

A special public lecture was held at Westminster in which 2,700 attended. Three lectures were given for the teachers unable to take the regular course and 1,500 attended. There were conferences, meetings and receptions at many of the major cities. Members of universities came to meet Montessori. Wherever she went she received a reception. Because of the enthusiasm in the United Kingdom, Montessori decided to conduct teacher training courses in England every two years from that year, 1919.

In May 1921, Lecture 14 of her training course in London, Montessori fully explained her didactic materials and how she expected them to be used. She emphasized the correct procedures to be followed in presenting the materials to children. 'First of all, let us consider the presentation of the material, which consists in using it in the precise way when placed in front of the child,' she told the trainees.

> In this particular case it consists of the displacing and replacing of certain objects. Sometimes the correct presentation of material requires the preparation of the individual. For instance, the preparation of the fingers for the tactile exercise, or the temporary impeding of some other sense, such as sight, may be required. Sometimes it is necessary to demonstrate a certain mode of procedure in the presentation, such as lightness of the hand in touching surfaces and the almost imperceptible movement of the hands when weighing the baric tablets.
>
> (Chattin-McNichols, 1992: 53–4)

It was neither a lesson nor a presentation, she insisted, more an initiation. 'So the teacher initiates the child,' she told the trainees:

> And it is almost as though she gives him a key to the secret of this modification or development of himself of which he is in need. We do not in effect teach him anything in the presentation; we are merely placing his feet upon the path which will lead him to his goal, which is perfection. In order that this material will have the desired effect, that is the child shall be stimulated to the exercise, it is necessary that the teacher should know the technique of correct presentation. (ibid.: 54)

Every piece of material for practical life and sensorial education was demonstrated in a slow, deliberate, exact manner.

Control of error

Most of the didactic material controlled every error because the child could self-correct. She observed that 'self-correction leads the child to concentrate his attention upon the differences of dimensions and compare the various pieces' (ibid.: 171). The psycho-sensory exercise lies in the comparison. Montessori observed and studied how much each child achieved. The didactic materials were not to test or measure but to enable observations to be made and studied.

In August, 1929, at the end of the teacher training course in Denmark, she announced her decision to form a parent body, the Association Montessori Internationale (AMI), to oversee activities in Montessori schools (Kramer, 1976: 305). The decision split Montessori followers in England. Groups who wished to preserve 'pure' Montessori education immediately joined AMI. Montessori was to be president and she chose Berlin as headquarters. In 1932, the first edition of *Peace and Education* was published by Montessori. In 1935, when Hitler closed Montessori schools, the headquarters of AMI moved to Amsterdam, where it remains to this day.

Montessori in Asia

In the Introduction to *The Discovery of the Child* (1967b) Montessori commented on the spread of Montessori education into Asia where schools had been established in Syria, India, China, Africa (from Egypt to the Cape), as well as in the United States, Canada and Latin America.

In 1939, she was invited by the Theosophical Society in England to visit India. When she and her son Mario were in India to give teacher training courses, the outbreak of World War II meant she was interned for the duration of the war, while Mario was imprisoned. He was released on 31 August 1940 by the Governor as a gift for Montessori's seventieth birthday, but they were not allowed to travel for the duration of the war. During these years, Montessori and Mario trained thousands of teachers who travelled far distances to attend the teacher training courses. Mahatma Ghandi visited Montessori several times. He had met her in Italy because he agreed with all her views on education as a vehicle to bring world peace through the education of young children. He was a visitor at several of her courses (Lawson, 1974: 36–49).

Montessori also met Krishnamurti during her stay in India. Both condemned traditional approaches to education (Currie and Breadmore, 1983).

Montessori education after World War II

On her return to Europe from India after World War II, Montessori conducted her first course for children from birth to 3 years in Rome in 1945. In 1946 she travelled to England where interest in Montessori had languished during her eight year absence (Cohen, 1974: 62). But she was met by faithful followers Margaret Homfray and Phoebe Child who had arranged a teacher training course (Kramer, 1976). After that, she travelled north to Edinburgh where she was presented with an Honorary Fellowship of the Educational Institute of Scotland (Prakasam, 1948). At the end of 1948 she returned to India for a planned opening of a Montessori University, but she was caught up in an enormous upheaval when huge numbers of people were journeying north to the newly created Pakistan (Potts, 1980: 40).

Montessori returned to the Netherlands and Amsterdam where Mario married and settled. By the 1950s, Cohen claims that in England 'she was quite forgotten' (Cohen, 1974: 62), but Montessori continued to return to England to conduct her teacher training courses since she remained the only person able to train teachers. In 1951, she addressed the Montessori Conference held in London. The following year, 1952, she died before her planned visit to Africa.

From 1908, Montessori saw the need for teachers to be trained. Her decision to do all the teacher training herself meant there were never enough teachers. That dilemma exists worldwide to this day.

Montessori and Child Development 4

> The laws of development are there, they have to be observed, ascertained and followed.
>
> (Montessori, 1974: 21)

Educators from the time of Plato have commented on child development including 'Rousseau, Pestalozzi, Owen and Spencer who were all *naturalistic* educators concerned with the child's nature, stages of human growth and development' (Boyd, 1921: 36) and there were similarities in their findings.

Throughout her lifetime, Montessori continued researching using as her basic tool objective, analytical, clinical observation. From the first experiment in the Casa dei Bambini, she conducted a *scientific* study of each child to explain his development. That essentially became the basis of Montessori education.

Development of the whole child is a key feature of Montessori education. Through observation Montessori discovered ways of helping development which were reported in *The Montessori Method* (1964), and in 1916, she noted that there was 'a simple and clearly defined difference between pedagogy and psychology' (Montessori, 1965b: 114). The essential difference was as follows:

- *Pedagogy* determines experimentally the means of development and the method of applying them while respecting the internal or personal liberty of the individual.
- *Psychology* studies average reactions or individual reactions in the species or the individual.

But, as she emphasized, 'the two things are two aspects of a single fact, which is *the development of man*' (ibid.).

For Montessori, it was an indisputable fact that everything in the universe worked according to the laws of nature, with regular cycles for all things in the cosmos – including human life. The rules of nature never changed, only varied. A pioneer of child development, she was interested in the development of the whole child (a personality), and as she had observed that all children passed through observable physical changes of natural development, she asked, 'Why should the covert human psyche be different?' Scientifically, she observed children within classroom settings and showed how every child passed through the same phases of psychic development but varied at a speed dependent on each child's intellect. She was able to show 'the general laws which govern the child's psychical health [having] their parallel in those of his physical health' (Montessori, 1965b: 1). She maintained that the inner changes of the child's covert psyche could be observed only through the physical changes in a child's behaviour while using a piece of didactic material, and those hidden psychic changes were as different as those visible changes in the cycle of a butterfly. By the 1930s, Montessori's continued observations were still not considered to be scientific.

Montessori education 'begins at birth and extends to under graduates using the same method' (Montessori, 1975: 3). Vital to note here is that the teacher (directress) must be sensitive to the psychic needs and the physical needs of each child at every stage of development. Montessori insisted that 'we must consider the human *personality* and not a method of education' and 'if the human personality is one (whole) at all stages of development we perceive a principle of education which has regard for all stages' (ibid.: 4, 5). Method was defined as 'help given in order that the human personality may achieve its independence' (ibid.).

Planes of development

Montessori's main aim was to help each child's natural development. From birth to adulthood the four planes of development described by Montessori are:

1. Birth to 6 years [sub-divided into 0–3 years; 3–6 years] an absorbent mind
2. 6 years to 12 years [sub-divided into 6–9 years; 9–12 years] a conscious mind
3. 12 years to 18 years [sub-divided into 12–15 years; 15–18 years] abstract thinking
4. 18 years to 24 years. Adulthood.

(Montessori, 1967a: 19)

These cycles, or planes of development, became the basis for multi-age grouping of children in Montessori education. Children on the same plane of development were placed in cycles (multi-age), remaining together for approximately 3 years. Montessori believed, 'official education has recognised these different psychological types'. Children from birth to 6 years were excluded from compulsory education. Primary school for children 6–12 years, and high school for adolescents were compulsory. She pointed out, 'only a psychological basis common to all children can have made possible this kind of school organization . . . but schools are insensitive to the needs of students, particularly at upper levels' (Montessori, 1939: 20, 21). She noted,

> We must consider the human personality as one at all stages of devel-
> opment. We perceive a principle of education which has regards for all
> stages of development which begins at birth and extends to undergradu-
> ates using the same method, love and respect.
>
> (Montessori, 1974: 5)

Understanding development of the whole child, a personality

From the perspective of formal education – infant, primary and secondary – a number of stages in child development were identified by
Montessori, all deserving of mention for their uniqueness in educational literature.

Birth to 3 years (infancy)

Known by Montessori as the sensory-motor period, this is the most
rapid period of development and the most important period in life
because during this period, 'the fundamental features of development
which characterise the human potential are established' (Montessori,
1948c: 90). It was not until the late 1930s that Montessori's observations of the first 3 years of life were published in *The Absorbent Mind*
(1967a). The newborn was recognized by Montessori as a 'psychic
embryo' (Montessori, 1973c: 23) who had had 'a psychic life before
birth' (Montessori, 1974: 22) but, she observed, attention was paid
immediately to the child's physical needs while the psychic needs
were neglected. She stressed the need to help psychic development
from the moment of birth because that was when *personality* began
to develop and the child 'has to *create* his personality' (Montessori,
1975: 67). Indeed it was essential that 'the first care of the newborn
babe . . . must be a care of his mental life, and not just his bodily life,
which is the rule today' (Montessori, 1967a: 61). From birth 'man's
intelligence is being formed, the full totality of his psychic powers'. For Montessori, the newborn child possessed *an unconscious*

absorbent mind which observed everything in the environment and 'brings about his marvellous progress' (ibid.: 21, 24) especially in the development of his personality. From birth to 2½ years the child was totally engrossed in self-development of his personality (Montessori, 1948c: 99). At this age he shows an interest in becoming social, and by 3 years the child has laid the foundations of his personality (Montessori, 1967a: 16). The child creates himself, his own distinctive character, intellect, will power, morals (ibid.: 175).

Movement, 'the motor functions by which he is to secure his balance and learn to walk and talk', could easily be observed (Montessori, 1965b: 34). Montessori recorded her observations that the child was able to select from his environment all he needed for his 'sensory functions' and his own development according to his own nature (ibid.: 34; Montessori, 1967a: 24). The *hand* was used unconsciously from birth which helped to develop the mind. The mind is hand made when the child makes discoveries with some *thing*. But although the child needed the greatest of help during the first period of life there could be *no direct adult influence* because the child developed through his own unconscious efforts and by nature's urge 'he absorbs impressions by life itself' (Montessori, 1967a: 18, 24). Each child constructed himself. He created his mind, his memory, his will, his power to reason and '*adapted* to the social environment in which character was formed' (ibid.: 28). Everything that would develop in future years was based on the foundations laid by the child during this first period of life. Adults could help simply by providing the correct conditions for the child to develop – rather than by determining and controlling the whole teaching-learning process.

Discovery and the sensitive periods

Observations from birth showed that children passed through what Montessori named *sensitive periods* at which times 'children were endowed with special psychic powers' (Montessori, 1978: 2). They had definite features which were central to Montessori education and were defined as being 'a predisposition to an area of growth' and transient in nature. They occurred for a few weeks (or months) when a child had an insatiable desire to acquire a skill. It was the child, guided from *within*, who decided when it was time to learn, and the learning was spontaneous. There was a sensitive time for the child to learn order, eye-hand coordination, sounds – but whatever was decided, the child was easily disposed to learn that particular skill at that particular time. If there were obstacles to the learning, the child became frustrated. As one sensitive period passed, another sensitive period emerged. If the skill was not learned during the sensitive period, the child may be required to learn it later at which time much effort was required, and the skill was then difficult to perfect (ibid.: 35–41). The example given by Montessori was the wild boy of Averyon who never learned to walk erect or speak in sentences because of the obstacles to his learning during the sensitive periods for such learning. It was important to have knowledge of the sensitive periods and their order of occurrence or 'one cannot understand the construction of the psyche of the child (Montessori, 1973c: 21). Montessori worked closely with parents and child carers so they would understand development because 'it was formerly thought that small children had no psyche life' while to Montessori 'the chief characteristic of a human babe is intelligence' (Montessori, 1974: 31). For continuity, home and school should provide similar living conditions. Children needed to be treated with respect and love. The different sensitive periods at each stage of development were to be taken into consideration in Montessori education.

Three years to six years (early childhood)

This was a period when the child still possessed *a unconscious absorbent mind* which 'is indeed a marvellous gift to humanity' (Montessori, 1973c: 28; 1975: 73) and is when 'he learns everything without knowing he is learning it', but 'slowly he passes little by little from the unconscious (mind) to the conscious (mind)' during this period of development (Montessori, 1967a: 26). At 3 years, on entry to a Children's House, observations of each child's activity showed the progress of each child's development. You can see 'that he is always playing with some *thing*. This meant he was working out, and making conscious something that his unconscious mind had earlier absorbed' (ibid.: 27). At this stage of development the child was always 'busy with his hands' and 'cannot think without his hands' (Montessori, 1973c: 63, 67). Movement and mind worked together. By 3 years 'the child thinks and reflects and *the hand* is directed by the child, only he can organize his psychic life' (Montessori, 1967a: 222). The child's mind had developed along with the power to understand the why, the how and the meaning of consequences.

Normalization

Montessori had mentioned in *The Montessori Method* (1964) that when a child concentrated on any piece of material there was an observable change in behaviour, there was a development *within* the child who then became calm and happy showing signs of inner peace and that the nervous system was rested. The change in behaviour appeared in every child in all four Children's Houses in 1909. Children's behaviour became *'normal'* in every Casa dei Bambini worldwide. Montessori claimed normal behaviour to be the way nature intended children to be. *'Normalized'* was the name Montessori gave later to free children who acted in a calm, self-disciplined manner, revealing their true personality. Free children made it possible for a teacher to observe 'the way in which children pass from the first disordered movements to those which are spontaneous and ordered' (Montessori, 1964: 94, 95). She spoke of normalization of child in *The Discovery of the Child* (1967b), in *The Secret of Childhood* (1936) and again in *The Absorbent Mind* (1967a) pointing out that it was possible for every child to become 'self disciplined through freedom', working with didactic materials and not being ordered to obey. The change 'does not happen gradually, but appears all of a sudden . . . in an environment prepared for him. It continues to happen today and it is possible to observe the change happening to a child. The *self-disciplined, normalized child* was to become the heart of Montessori education'.

The normalized child possessed hidden inner powers. The discovery of this *inner child*, Montessori maintained, was part of nature waiting to be discovered. Understanding her method, was to see it as 'the consequence of having *assisted the development* of psychological phenomena which had remained unobserved and hence unknown for thousands of years'. She had chanced upon it because she 'taught little and observed much' (Montessori, 1967b: 326).

The scientist, a discoverer, Montessori explained, 'has the power to reproduce the conditions for the repetition of the phenomena he has seen. He does so because he understands what produces them.' Once deviant to normal behaviour has been witnessed, 'these psychological phenomena could not be passed by'. She 'was filled with the desire to see if it was possible to have them repeated' (Association of Montessorians, 1961). She claimed that it was partly by chance, partly her scientific preparation and previous work with children which enabled her and her trained teachers to reproduce the same learning conditions. Changes in children's behaviour were always the same: children became *normalized.*

Montessori talked and wrote about the normalized child for nearly 50 years. She spoke about how children 'reveal a different nature to the one he had been previously known by', and how she had observed that the nature of children's behaviour changed from *deviant to normal* when they were given freedom.

Two natures of childhood

By the 1930s, Montessori explained in more detail how to distinguish the two natures of childhood: deviant and normal. She described '*a view of childhood* that had not been known before' and she stressed that 'the foundations of all that we are doing consists of being able to distinguish between the *two natures of the child*' (Montessori Course, London, 1933) which Montessori claimed was *her greatest discovery*. She had 'discovered a hidden child, a hidden man, a buried human being who must be liberated'.

1. *Deviants*, Montessori explained, were children whose true course of development had been blocked by adults. Before 3 years there had been obstacles to spontaneous activity caused by lack of freedom. The danger was that if deviations were not fixed, they became fixed in the character for life. In general, children with deviations fall into three categories:

- *Strong* children were rebels who fought back against adults; sometimes had violent tantrums, were defiant, cruel; identified as 'bad'.
- *Weak* children had given up the fight and were submissive; quiet; often labelled 'good' except for some who lied.
- *Bright* children were highly imaginative, intelligent, possessed good language skills; restless with poor control of movements; had chosen not to fight and not to give in.

Montessori pointed out that members of society were so used to some of these abnormal behaviours that they applauded and even valued some of those traits. For example, the quiet, submissive child was 'good' and the imaginative 'bright' child who described incredible things or creatures, was seen to possess a valuable trait even though his 'company was none too agreeable' (Montessori, 1978: 170–85; 1967a: 192–201). But Montessori maintained *all deviations could be cured*. She observed 'the visible disappearance of these defects in children as soon as they found themselves in a place where active experience . . . and free exercise of their powers could *nourish* their minds' (Montessori, 1967a: 199). When children could concentrate 'and focus their minds on something of real interest to them, their defects disappeared' (ibid.). All deviations 'came from a single cause, which was *insufficient nourishment* for *the life of the mind* ' (the spirit). The conversion process could be suddenly and easily observed. The child became *normalized*.

2. *Normal children* show true, natural characteristics, and for Montessori a good character was the birthright of every child. 'Normal behaviour' was recognized in a child who was calm, self-controlled, willing, obedient, affectionate, cheerful and lively. Such a child enjoyed stillness and being independent of adults. It was and has remained the aim that every child in a Casa dei Bambini becomes normal by 6 years; this remains the main aim today.

A normalized child gained self-control, therefore punishments were not required, and he refused prizes because the inner joy and happiness was reward enough. When a child stopped looking for a reward or praise, it was a sign of a leap in development. Freedom led children to self-discipline and become masters of themselves.

Montessori education spread rapidly, and reports of normalized children in Montessori environments were received from Montessori schools on every continent. She wrote that 'normalization was repeated unfailingly in all our schools with children belonging to different social classes, races and civilizations. *It is the most important result of our whole work*' and normalization was 'the child's contribution to society' (Montessori, 1967a: 201, 204).

With the success of Montessori's early work, by 1909 tributes were forthcoming from some of her medical peers. Dr Crichton Miller reported at the time 'that doctors of medicine and professors of psychology were saying her work would eventually make nerve specialists superfluous and if the Montessori method was established in all schools, almshouses will have to be established for psychologists' (Kramer, 1976: 264). In Montessori's own words:

> I was made to realise that certain conditions which fulfilled psychic needs had evidently also influence upon the physical body . . . health and happiness were closely linked and the time came when doctors recommended our Case dei Bambini as a sort of health resort.
>
> (Montessori Course, London, 1933)

Implications for research

Practical life and sensorial materials

Montessori's practical life materials from 1907 were intended for motor education leading each child to become self-controlled. Simple activities such as caring for the environment and care of self were emphasized. She emphasized that free movement was synonymous with 'spontaneous development' (Montessori, 1964: 230). At a course in 1942, Montessori stressed that the selection of 'material in our schools today is based on the selection that the children have voluntarily made . . . from the things they had at their disposal' which 'brought us to the conception that there *must be just that amount and no more*'. The selection of materials 'was proved by the children' to be their choice. When Montessori modified Itard's sensorial materials, it was always the purpose that it would attract children's attention. What always attracted interest, attention and concentration were objects which could be moved, be made and unmade and be displaced and replaced. Such objects 'made prolonged occupation possible' (Montessori, 1967a: 123).

Always concerned about psychic life, Montessori averred, 'the organization of psychic life begins with the characteristic phenomenon of *attention*' (Montessori, 1965b: 156). She was able to show that young children had long attention spans. No child in a Montessori environment suffered from Attention Deficit Disorder (ADD).

Attention and information processing

It was Donald Broadbent (1958) who produced one of the earliest models of information processing which was a *theory of attention* to explain what happened in listening tasks. By the 1970s an affiliation grew from findings of behaviourists, learning theorists, cognitive psychologists, developmentalists and researchers of information processing. Learning theorists now allowed for the existence of *thought*. The information processing approach influenced the fields of cognitive psychology and cognitive development. Researchers were concerned with what goes on in children's minds. They researched how children learned and remembered. They maintained that processing began in each learners' senses followed by attention to the task. The learner worked and thought in what was called Short Term Memory (STM) 'with seven pieces of information, plus or minus two' (Miller, 1956), and if the learner had the opportunity to practise (repeat), the new information was learned and stored in Long Term Memory (LTM) (Gage and Berliner, 1979: 104–314; Clarke-Stewart et al., 1985: 252, 353).

A decade later the Interactive Model of information processing was introduced. This model attempted to integrate two components, learning and information processing. Developmental psychologists Brown et al. (1983) developed this model which considered the interaction among the activities of the learner, characteristics of the learner, nature of the materials to be learned and qualities of the task by which the learning was assessed. This model more closely matched Montessori education, which considered every aspect which affected the learner, than the Stimulus/Response model put forth by psychologists in 1907 when the first Casa dei Bambini opened.

A second discovery

The second major discovery made by Montessori in the first Casa dei Bambini was that children learned to write and read spontaneously when didactic materials for language development were introduced into the environment (Montessori, 1964: 291, 296). The *discovery* that the sensory period for beginning to write and read was 4 years brought attention to the first Casa in 1907. This spontaneous acquisition of culture (writing and reading) was made possible because the child still possessed an absorbent mind and was given specially designed Montessori didactic materials which helped each child to teach himself (ibid.: 5). The discovery showed that 'the mind of a child is capable of acquiring culture at an incredibly early age, through own unaided activity' (ibid.: 71). At that time children 4 years to 6 years were considered to be 'too young for school to be taught, and teaching was identified with education' (Montessori, 1974: 25). Montessori had shown these prejudices to be wrong. The child also had adapted to the social conditions of the school which were democratic, where he was respected and had rights. Also, he mastered the environment. The aim of education during this period was for every child to become independent of the adult (Montessori, 1973c: 33). By the sixth year the absorbent mind began gradually to fade and observations showed that there was 'psychologically, a decided change in personality' (Montessori, 1961: 4).

When Montessori began her first experiment in the first Casa dei Bambini, she stated 'child psychology does not exist' and used the definition of Wundt that 'all methods of experimental psychology may be reduced to one; namely, carefully recorded observation of the subject' (Montessori, 1964: 72, 73). After 40 years of observation and research in child development, Montessori wrote, 'it was this early research which led to the foundation of child psychology' (Montessori, 1974: 107). In the future there was a need for

> more research and more investigations to discover the mysteries and hidden powers of the children . . . the energies and powers embodied in a tiny little child are more powerful than the newly discovered energy of the atomic bomb.
>
> (Montessori, 1974: 72)

6–12 years (childhood)

In 1910, Montessori started her observations of children aged 6–12 years and her findings were published in two large volumes – *The Advanced Montessori Method*, Volumes 1 and 2, published in English in 1916. Montessori described the child at 6 years as being 'a different child who presents characteristics different to those he exhibited during preceding years'; indeed the child at each stage of development changed and the change could be compared to a kind of 'metamorphoses' (Montessori, 1975: 3). There was 'a great transformation at six years . . . the psychic entity begins to become approachable' (Montessori, 1978: 14) because the absorbent mind had faded. Throughout her writings, Montessori noted that during the childhood years there was a calm growth due to relative physical and mental stability described as a period with 'no transformations, a time of serenity and docility' (ibid.: 15). At 6 years the normalized child 'is calm and happy' (Montessori, 1967a: 19). Childhood was a period when there was an interest in culture and morals. The child wished to use his own judgement which often differed from the teacher's (Montessori, 1961: 5). The psychological (inner) change that had taken place 'shows in the hunger for knowledge plus a claim to mental independence' (ibid.: 6). This was the time when there was 'a need for abstraction, and intellectual activity makes itself felt about the seventh year' (Montessori, 1975: 5) and the mind 'bases itself on imagination which needs to be built and organized' (ibid.: 38). The children judged the acts of others and wanted to know 'what has been done well or poorly' (ibid.: 11). It is the age when 'the sensitive period of the concept of *justice* is born' which 'form the *interior*' along with the 'injustice and legal right concept' (ibid.: 12, 13). Education at this stage needed to present 'the natural sense of true justice' which differed from 'distributive justice about individual rights' (ibid.: 13). Moral relationships awakened and children 'do not wish to offend' (ibid.: 18). *Social* interests developed in children. They showed that they wanted to become part of a social group within the classroom and a team outside the classroom. At a higher level they had an interest in 'aiding the weak, aged and sick (ibid.: 6, 17). The child needed 'wider boundaries for his social experiences' and 'scouting has brought an organized form of life to children' (Montessori, 1975: 9, 11). Scouting meant membership of a society which had a social and moral aim. Children joined and freely chose to obey principles (ibid.: 18, 19). The mind was at an abstract level which 'discovers causes' and the child 'views things in entirety' so everything in the universe needed to be shown to be interrelated. Montessori suggested much work could be done outside the classroom at this stage. The great outdoors demanded more adaptation and a new environment to be mastered.

12 to 15 years (adolescence)

Montessori stressed this was a very special stage of development and 'from a psychological viewpoint this is a critical age'. It was a time of great physical change and therefore of great psychological change. The young adolescent, needed as much special care as a newborn child. He needed less physical exercise, needed less intellectual work (Montessori, 1975: 101). Early puberty could be a dangerous time during which mental health was seldom recognized by schools which 'need to reform' (ibid.: 97). Children had attended Primary School for years and had their errors corrected, been punished, rewarded, were not allowed to talk or help each other in class every day for years and neither were they recognized nor treated as human beings. Now in adolescence, they felt humiliated, guilty as though they had committed crimes – 'brotherhood was not born' (Montessori, 1967a: 240). There were 'doubts and hesitations, violent emotions, discouragements and an unexpected decrease of intellectual capacity occurs' and 'the difficulty of studying was due to a psychological characteristic of this age'. All of a sudden the adolescent became 'very sensitive to the rudeness and humiliations he had previously suffered with patient indifference' and reactions 'are often rebellious' (Montessori, 1975: 101). Physical health during puberty also was seldom recognized as such, especially by schools (Montessori, 1967a: 19). Montessori suggested that Secondary Schools 'need to reform' (Montessori, 1948c: 97).

There was however 'one thing that education can take as a sure guide and that is *the personality* of the children who are to be educated' (ibid.: 99). Montessori urged that the psychological needs of children in this age group must be addressed. They needed to live in a stress free environment with no stress of examinations. Montessori's vision of future education was noted in the preface of *From Childhood to Adolescence* (1975: xiv).

> My vision of the future is no longer of people taking exams and proceeding on that certification from secondary school to university, but of individuals passing from one stage of independence to a higher, by means of their own activity, through their own effort of will, which constitutes the inner evolution of the individual.

Adolescents often found stressful living conditions at home, and Montessori warned parents what happened to children growing under such conditions. These 'unloved, abandoned, forgotten children organized themselves into gangs in rebellion against authority and adult made regulations' (ibid.: 235). She was mindful of the prisoners she had interviewed and studied as a medical student.

Montessori suggested that adolescents be moved into a kind of boarding school situation which would cater for students' needs by providing correct living conditions and with no academic pressures. Conflict with parents would be avoided for those who did not understand development during this period of life. The boarding school called Erdkinder (land children) would help young adolescents to become economically independent through their own labour. Ways of becoming financially independent included working the land, running part of the school like a hotel where parents could visit and pay for their accommodation while students learned everything required to run a hotel with a restaurant. Another suggestion was a shop where students could sell farm produce and their own art and craft products.

15–18 years (adolescence/youth)

This was the final period of development before adulthood. These years were calmer, and students were better able to study than during the first period of adolescence (Montessori, 1948c: 101). But if adolescents, at 16 years, 'are treated like babies, with petty threats of bad marks on which their future depends', they often had 'bitter rebellious feelings which gave rise to amoral characteristics, sometimes criminality' (ibid.). Serious study could be taken up by those who wished to enter university. Those students who had to prepare for entry into universities were helped and guided by the teacher. They must prepare themselves for the unforeseen, unexpected trials of life which 'no one can prepare us directly to meet: it is only a vigorous spirit (mind) that can be prepared for everything' (Montessori, 1916: 168). It was essential for students to understand that 'life must not remain an unknown quantity . . . for success in life in every case depends on self-confidence and knowledge of one's own capacity' (Montessori, 1975: 102). Success also 'depended on the ability to adapt' (Montessori, 1964: 271), as '*adaptation* is the most essential quality: for the progress of the world is continually opening up new careers' (ibid.: 99). Montessori's hope was for each adolescent to reach his potential and take his place as a contributing member of society. It 'is necessary that the human potential (personality) should be prepared for the unforseen' (ibid.: 49). At 18 years, Montessori students were prepared to adapt to future changes in technology and in society. When has it been more important to be able to adapt than in these new times of technology and globalization? Montessori warned about man's inability to keep up with the technological age in *Education for a New World* (Montessori, 1946c).

Connectionists – how children learn

Montessori was completely out of step with Connectionists and the theories of the day. While she always 'proceeded from the child himself' (Montessori, 1948c: 25), her contemporaries had continued working on their own theories. Some merit mention to illustrate the difference.

The Connectionists theories were informed by research on animals. Classical Conditioning theory was introduced by Pavlov (1849–1936). His research findings recorded responses made by dogs to a stimulus. John Watson (1878–1958) continued his work applying Classical Conditioning to children. The method was extreme. His method was to prove that children could be conditioned to fear something that had previously been a neutral object. The work of Edwin Guthrie (1896–1959) researched the practical application of the principles to learning. He followed the stimulus/response theory but added, 'What we do is what we learn' (Guthrie, 1952: 23). Edward Thorndike (1874–1949) showed in his research that rewards meant a certain behaviour would be repeated while punishments suppressed behaviour. His findings were published in *Principles of Teaching Based upon Psychology* (Thorndike, 1906: 5). To him, research should discover what learners do, not what they feel. It was B. F. Skinner (1904–90) who introduced Operant Conditioning in the 1930s which emphasized the importance of reinforcement by rewards and punishments. His research was done with rats.

Connectionists were concerned with learning where children were perceived as passive non-thinkers being stimulated from the outside. The method was whole class teaching and every student was working on the same task at the same time and given the same amount of time to complete work. Children were expected to learn by rote. This view of learning has had great impact on education especially in the Primary School years. It remained in many teacher training courses until the early 1960s. Reinforcement style of teaching/learning could still be found in schools in the 1990s. Children continue to be threatened with punishments and expulsion from school. In 1924, a strong stance was taken by Lev Vygotsky (1896–1934) 'against Pavlov's dominating theory of conditioning reflexes and he called for the recognition of man's conscious behaviour' (Wertsch, 1985: 8). Vygotsky, a Russian psychologist, became 'the darling of the intellectual community' (Lohmann, 1988: 4). Lohmann suggests that Vygotsky may have been aware of *The Montessori Method*, translated into Russian in 1912, when a Montessori classroom was set up in the Tsar's palace in Petersburg for the royal children. Certainly the position Vygotsky took in his stance against Pavlov matched the stance taken earlier by Montessori in 1907 as did the fact that they both agreed on the importance of man's consciousness. Montessori was unaware of Vygotsky's work which was not published in the West until 23 years after her death.

Intelligence testing

At the turn of the twentieth century Alfred Binet had been working on how to measure intelligence. Montessori noted 'the Simon-Binet tests can neither measure anything nor give an approximate idea of intellectual level of intelligence according to age', and she also queried 'whether *response* was due to intrinsic activity or individual action on environment' (Montessori, 1965b: 111). Binet believed he was measuring intelligence which he defined as being a general ability to learn, to reason, to grasp concepts and to deal with abstractions (Binet and Simon, 1905).

Montessori was opposed to intelligence tests, which meant she also challenged the idea of the constant IQ. She had already demonstrated with children found in asylums (1898–1900) that children's intelligence could be raised (Hunt, 1964). To Montessori, the *inner* child, a personality, could not be divided into parts, nor could intelligence be tested. Intelligence tests, told nothing of a child's personality, only told how he did on that particular test on that day.

Critics and supporters

Support was slow in coming, but in the late 1930s, Skeels and Dye 'virtually proved the malleability of the intelligence and the unreliability of IQ scores with regard to the environmental experience . . . and were pilloried by the academic establishment' (Lohmann, 1988:

7). In more recent times, Howard Gardner (1983) identified multiple intelligences: linguistic, logical-mathematical, special, kinaesthetic, musical, interpersonal and intrapersonal. He has added naturalistic (exploring nature) intelligence to the list and is presently working on spiritual intelligence (Schiller, 2000). Note that spiritual development was the first consideration in Montessori education. At birth the child was a 'spiritual embryo'. The spirit was the life of the mind and was the interaction of all the intelligences mentioned by Gardner which when combined made up each child's personality and that was what Montessori sought to develop in her holistic approach to education – a personality. When she spoke to a child, it was to the whole child – a personality. In 1983, Gardner also wrote that intelligent tests were 'limited not only in competences that they examine but in the ways they examine them' (in Courts, 1997: 101). In her well-known article *Kid Watching: An Alternative to Testing*, Yetta Goodman (1987) concurred in the view that *observation* was an alternative to testing 80 years after Montessori.

Many critics of Montessori education began in 1907 when children in the first Casa dei Bambimi began to read and write. Psychologists questioned her spectacular results with young children aged 4 years beginning to write and read. They 'questioned if the mental life of the child ought not to be immolated in favour of useless results because a little later on, a child over six years of age can learn to read and write' (Montessori, 1948c: 22). But it was the criticisms of psychologist Charlotte Bühler who claimed 'mental faculties of children under five years of age are impermeable to any form of culture' (ibid.). Official education 'put our work aside' and primary teachers worked with children of 6 years and failed to arouse interest in children to learn to read. A reason for failing was that by 6 years they were no longer in the sensitive period for beginning to learn to read. Montessori's materials were designed for children to learn to read at 4 years and with successful results. The other researchers, Montessori recalled, continued 'to be concerned *not* with the inner patterns or powers of the mind but concentrated on external activities' (Montessori, 1974: 108). The 'miracle' of children learning to read spontaneously at 4 years was 'relegated to oblivion' and 'left to *me* to investigate the secrets of child psychology' (ibid.: 23). Montessori had found herself alone among psychologists with no support for her work from any of them.

More than 30 years later in 1939, Montessori wrote that 'psychologists were starting to concentrate on the development of the very young from the very earliest stage' and among them was Charlotte Bühler (Montessori, 1967a: 4) who must have changed her mind about the ability of young children.

At the end of her first book *The Montessori Method* (1964), in which she had recorded all her observations and discoveries in the first Casa, she hoped others would continue with classroom research and stated:

> It is my hope that, stating from the individual study of the child to be educated with our method, other educators will set forth the results of their experiments. These are the pedagogical books which await us in the future. (ibid.: 373)

Developmental theories

By the middle of the twentieth century a number of theories of development did appear. Among these were the theories of development proposed by past students of Montessori education including Jean Piaget, Erik Erikson and Lawrence Kohlberg. Jean Piaget changed from studying animals to studying children after he heard Montessori speak at a lecture. In the 1930s he became President of the Swiss Montessori Association (Montessori Jr, 1976: 65). He was a trained observer who believed children passed through periods of development, hierarchical periods by age. In the first period, the sensori-motor period, children showed their intelligence through activity with concrete materials. These could be observed easily. A unit of knowledge (a mental structure) was called a scheme. When more knowledge was assimilated the schemes changed and grew. Piaget's theories became popular in the 1960s when his writings were published in English. So much of Piaget's theory matches Montessori's findings, even the language used to describe his findings was similar. However, Montessori and Piaget had parted at least 20 years before publication of his work when she discovered his research was done using his own children on a one-to-one basis and not in a social classroom setting. Another point she strongly disagreed with was his method of including long, involved questions. Montessori believed in *few words* and she expected the children to ask the questions. In the United States, curriculum developers used Piaget's theory of cognitive development as their base, designing plans of work to match the achievement levels he had observed children reached at certain ages (Mussem, 1970). This was ironic when it was in the United States that William Heard Kilpatrick, half a century earlier, had dismissed Montessori education as having nothing new. There was always *a gap* between Piaget's theory and practice. It was Margaret Donaldson, a psychologist, who worked with Piaget in Switzerland, who was able to show why the findings of his experiments were not true because they were based on language which the children misunderstood (Donaldson, 1978).

Erik Erikson was a student of Montessori and had first met her when she presented a Montessori course in his native Denmark and later in Vienna where he lived with his wife. Both were supporters of Montessori education, and when they moved to the United States they set up a Montessori classroom in their home. They were among the party to greet Montessori on her first visit to the United States in 1913. Erikson developed a theory of Personality Development which echoes some of Montessori's writings on the development of personality.

Lawrence Kohlberg, who studied under Montessori, developed a theory of Moral Development and there has been controversy about his work, too. Anna Freud, daughter of Sigmund Freud, was a staunch Montessori supporter. She was able to demonstrate how the two doctors, Freud and Montessori, agreed on findings about *the importance of the first 3 years of life* and how early experiences were related to disturbances of the mind later in life. Freud's interest always remained studying adults, connecting their disturbed minds to experiences during early childhood. Montessori continued to study children in classrooms and worked to remove deviations found in children during early childhood. 'Normalization' ensured they would lead happy, normal lives later. None of these psychologists supporting Montessori conducted their research within classrooms and did not provide practical classroom experiences to help children develop. All their names were known to students of education but Montessori's name was not. Two practising Scottish teachers who studied under Montessori produced practical exercises developed from their own classroom observations. Margaret Drummond's books for mathematics and Elizabeth Ruxton's ideas for early literacy were found in many Scottish schools from the 1930s to 1960s. It was classroom teachers like these whom Montessori wanted to become researchers.

Implications for education

Montessori education was child centred which meant that each unique child required individual teaching to match his stage of development. The point is raised by James McVicker Hunt in his 1961 Introduction to *The Montessori Method*:

> When I wrote *Intelligence and Experience* this problem of match loomed as a large obstacle in the way of maximizing intelligent potential.
>
> (Introduction Montessori Method, 1964: xxviii)

A colleague had advised him to look up Montessori who had 'a solution to your problem of match – not a theoretical solution but a practical one'. He found Montessori education *did* offer a solution to breaking 'the lock-step' method of teaching and having children of different age groups in one class, selecting their own tasks led him 'to believe there is an important psychological basis for Montessori's practice' (ibid.: xxix).

In 1942 at a Montessori course in India, Montessori spoke of three trials to introduce Individualized Education into schools which were often confused with the Montessori method.

1) *The Individual Method* which was introduced in the United States by Helen Parkhurst, a former student of Montessori education. The system was to have as few students as possible, about seven students for one teacher so individualized instruction was possible. It was a system where the teacher chose what the students studied and so 'followed the old system' to some extent. Montessori pointed out to students that this individual method 'was thought as an improvement on ours and something more scientific' but in Montessori education 'individual education is included in our environment . . . based on free choice of the child' (Montessori Course, India, 1942).

2) *The Decroly Method* which was introduced by Ovide Decroly (1871–1932) in Belgium and Switzerland towards the end of his life. He showed the power of free choice although he had not agreed with it earlier in his career. He believed that the interest of children could be aroused by the teacher providing 'centres of interest' within the classroom. Montessori pointed out that these teacher chosen centres were to hold the interest of the whole class throughout the whole year. The teacher also instructed the children and was 'therefore based on the old plan'. Montessori averred that in Montessori education 'it is not the teacher who gives the product of our deductions, it is the child' (ibid.).

3) *Individual Work* which was devised by a former (unnamed) student of Montessori. The children did choose their own material to work with but much was brought from home. The children *were occupied* all day through with things that interested them, but Montessori pointed out that 'the children did not attain 'cultural development'. That is, they did not learn to write or read as children in a Montessori environment 'because there was no connection between the different activities within the classroom', and as a result the children always remained in 'a pre-elementary stage'. The child simply passed from 'one thing to another with no relation to his studies' (ibid.).

The final word on these three innovations belong to Montessori who observed that the main difference between them and the Montessori Method was that 'in our method . . . culture is developed upon systematic individual work which has as its basis individual *interest*' (ibid.).

There have been other schemes for individual methods including *Individual Programmed Learning*. One proponent was B. F. Skinner who continued his work on operant behaviour, using stimulus/ response, for over 40 years. He designed work which was graded into such small learning steps that students always succeeded. His programme allowed children to work at their own speed but they could *not miss a step*. It relied on the old lock-step method. He described this work in 1963 as being the process of programming knowledge and skills as the construction of carefully arranged sequences which led to objectives (Skinner, 1963: 169). About the same time John Carroll attributed learning to the *attitude* of the child along with the quality of instruction. He believed that if a child was allowed all the time he required to complete a task he would be successful (Carroll, 1963: 725). The problem for the teacher lay in organizing the classroom to allow each student the time he required to complete a task.

Implications for research

The study of child development by Montessori followed 'only one line of development which is normality' (Montessori Course, London: 1946). A developmental research project was reported by Avshalom Caspi in 1999. His longitudinal study asked, 'Are behavioural differences – or styles – fleeting qualities or do they presage (predict) the life patterns to follow?'

The study conducted by Phil Silva in Dunedin, New Zealand, was an investigation of the health, development and behaviour of children born between 1 April 1972 and 31 March 1973. Data was collected on birthdays of children at ages of 3, 5, 7, 9, 11, 13, 15, 18 and 21 in clinical one-to-one conditions.

The Dunedin study began in 1975 when children then aged 3 years participated in a 90-minute one-to-one test session. The test involved cognitive and motor tasks, picture vocabulary, fine and gross motor coordination. The researchers found on the basis of behavioural observations that the children could be classified into five distinct groups:

1) Well-adjusted type – self-controlled, self-confident, faced new people/situations
2) Uncontrolled type – impulsive, restless, distractible, labile emotional responses
3) Inhibited type – socially reticent, fearful, easily upset by strangers
4) Confident type – zealous, eager to explore materials, adjusted to testing situation
5) Reserved type – timid, cautious, uncomfortable in testing session.

The last two groups were excluded from analysis.

Data showed that at 18 years,

1) well-adjusted children maintained their behaviour style and had remained the same.
2) uncontrolled children described themselves as reckless, careless and enjoyed dangerous and exciting activities.
3) inhibited children described reported they were cautious, had little desire to influence others. They were described by the researchers as over-controlled and non-assertive.

The study was also reported by Yvonne Martin who stated 'the long-term child development study shows that by three years old, it is possible to predict the adult s/he will become' and programmes which 'try to curb anti-social behaviour in school-aged children may be far too late' (Martin, 1999).

The critical difference between the researchers of the Dunedin study and Montessori's observations is that Montessori education offers *a cure* for deviant behaviour in childhood, with the resultant change from deviant to normal behaviour continuing into adulthood. Researchers and psychologists today who work with children with behavioural disorders may find some useful 'cures' for children in Montessori education.

Education as development

In England, Geva Blenkin and Vicki Kelly (1996) were working with a group of researchers and teachers at Goldsmith's College who proposed a new form of Early Childhood education, an education which was developmentally appropriate and which required a developmentally appropriate curriculum. They viewed 'education as development' which could be based on the neo-Piagetian Theory and had taken years to develop. Advocates of 'education as development' aver that 'one of the most neglected aspects of school is the creation of an environment . . . and those who teach older children consider the classroom environment is of no importance at all' (Blenkin and Kelly, 1996: 1). Montessori reminded teachers that 'preparing the environment for normal healthy development is difficult but was needed at all stages of development' (Montessori, 1974: 97).

Many aspects of 'education as development' match Montessori education. These include:

- understanding child development
- commitment to child-centredness
- experiences which promote development
- procedural principles by which we should live founded in the notion of human development
- curriculum founded in human development and based on the needs and interests of pupils
- helping students to think for themselves
- process of development based at every stage by reference to intrinsic principles rather than external aims
- the child is an active learner educated through first hand experiences
- the teacher intervenes in each child's learning and development by providing experiences which help development
- human learning and development seen as qualitatively distinct from that of animals

- some experiences to be selected and presented in order, to support learning
- modern technology has shown that very young babies endeavour to make sense of their environment and self-direct control over it from the moment of birth (Bower, 1971)
- the need for a stimulating and challenging environment from a very young age the child's intellectual life is a good deal more sophisticated than once was thought
- key of abstract thinking is to refer to thinking back to concrete situations so abstract thinking and concrete experiences are permanently linked
- promote child's ability to think, support or 'scaffold' thinking and ability to think in abstract forms are not left to chance
- a more sophisticated view of human development does not separate the psychomotor and the affective from the cognitive
- recent research in a genuinely child-centred approach offers advice on how to select content of children's education by reference to the children themselves. (Blenkin and Kelly, 1996: xiii–27)

The special features of 'education as development' suggested by the researchers at Goldsmith College are very close to the special features of Montessori education although there are points of departure. Only two are mentioned here. The main difference is that there is still a gap between neo-Piagetian theory and practice which is not found in Montessori education because she began with practice and theory was developed later. The other difference is that 'education for development' is a psychological theory and not an educational theory. Kieran Egan's research points out the radical difference between a psychological theory and an educational theory. A psychological theory has '*a set of skills*' as the end product while an educational programme 'must be informed by the polis the child is being prepared to inhabit, or change, and the end product must be "*a recognisable person*"' (Egan, 1983: 115, 116). Montessori education does help prepare each student for the unforseen trials of life, as a self-confidant, responsible youth who knows his own worth, is willing to contribute to society and has an ability to adapt to any change or challenge in life.

Implications for research

It was not until the 1990s that researchers and commentators began writing about infants possessing an absorbent mind, passing through sensitive periods and becoming a normalized child. Marylyn Adams refers to 'a normalized child who is not some putatively "model" child we need to make explicit' (Adams, 1991: 211). James Gee spoke of Discourses (social encounters) where it was 'a usually taken for granted and tacit "theory" of what counts as a "normal" person and the right way to think, feel and behave' (Gee, 1996: 20). Muspratt et al. (1997) have key questions about *normalativity*. They ask, 'What prescriptive model of the literate person should any approach to critical literacy aspire to and can such a model be constructed?'

Carole Edelsky (1999) asks whole language teachers, 'What kind of students do we wish to create? and, What kind of society do we wish to have?'

Mobility of attention is endemic today. As early as 2001, it was reported that 11.2 per cent of Australian children reported as suffering from mental illnesses were being treated for attention deficit hyperactive disorder (ADHD) while 40 per cent were reported to suffer from anxiety, aggression and poor social interaction. These disturbing figures were issued by the national Survey of Mental Health, 2001. Doctors in Australia at that time were prescribing 50 million pills a year to calm children suffering from ADHD (Duffy, 2001). Professor Barry Nurcombe, child and adolescent psychologist, Queensland University, warned that there was 'potential for even greater problems if children were not treated early on, including suicide, substance abuse and criminal behaviour' (Hart, 2001). His greatest fears have been realized.

Montessori issued similar warnings in 1939, that any child, 'who is not protected with a view to his normal formation will later avenge himself on society by means of the adult who is formed by him' (Montessori, 1967a: 71).

Developmental curriculum

Montessori called great changes to the content of the curriculum. It was not to be what adults thought ought to be included but was to be based on the interests of individual children who were interested in everything. The content of the curriculum was to be wide and more varied. All learning was aimed to help and promote the development of the child. The fact that children thought differently at each stage of development had to be considered, especially when what a child learned depended on his experiences during every previous stage of development. By 1910, Montessori was trialling materials for children aged 6–12 years, and she wrote about children 3–6 years that 'small children are able to *do* things far above expected capacity' (Montessori, 1961: 108, 109). So she experimented by putting more and more challenging materials into Cycle 1 (3–6 years) noting that a young child accepted everything 'if it was put in an accepted manner, suited to the child's psychology' (Montessori, 1974: 28).

At 3 years Montessori children were introduced to all branches of culture: Language, Mathematics, History, Geography, Science, Art and Music. At a teacher training course Montessori averred that 'we must enlarge the syllabus' and by doing so 'we enlarge the mind' (Montessori Course, London, 1946). The materials were *not* the curriculum; it was the *interests* of the children which decided the curriculum. Each child's personality was different and complex and the curriculum had to match each child's stage of development.

Imagination, fantasy and creativity

Imagination had a sensory base as well as a solid foundation with sensorial materials (Montessori, 1964: 168) and was invaluable for children to learn anything that was not within sight. It helped each child to understand any topic based on reality, that is, truth.

'Imagination is a tool to discover the truth' (Montessori, 1967a: 161) and was important because:

1) it was a higher mental function
2) it helped children develop mentally
3) it had a role in the creative aspects of science and art (ibid.: 186).

For Montessori, there were two types of imagination to be considered:

- creative imagination in science was extrapolation from truth
- creative imagination of art was extrapolation from the senses (ibid.: 189).

In her writings, Montessori gives many examples of children revealing their powers of imagination. One example was when she introduced a globe, 'the world', for the first time. A 3 year old looked at the globe, declaring after a moment that he now understood what his uncle meant when he said he had been around the world three times. He had grasped that the globe was a model. The child showed he was able 'to form the idea' that the globe represented the world and she concluded that was only possible by 'virtue of an intangible power of his mind, an imaginative power' (ibid.: 176). Imagination was 'a great gift' (ibid.: 177), and it could help young children understand ideas and concepts and bring them to a level of abstraction (Montessori, 1975: 38). However, she maintained that there was a great difference between imagination and fantasy.

Fantasy confused with imagination

In 1939 Montessori wrote about fantasy and that it must not be confused with imagination. Fantasy was 'unconnected mental images and allowed the mind to wander rather than become ordered' (Montessori, 1967a: 189). She wondered why adults told children fairy stories, because if they could imagine fairies and fairyland 'it is not difficult for a child to imagine America' (Montessori, 1975: 176, 177).

Fantasy confused the child and his mind wandered. It impeded development and was not to be confused with extrapolation from the truth. It did not help the child gain a realistic view of his environment and hindered his perception and understanding of the world. Adults often confused imagination and fantasy and did not discriminate between the two.

Montessori clarified the point that a child's mentality differed from that of an adult. A child 'escapes from our strongly marked and restricted limits, and loves to wander in the fascinating worlds of unreality' a tendency 'characteristic of savage peoples' who are attracted to 'the supernatural and the unreal' (ibid.). A form of this kind of imagination was 'universally recognised as creative imagination . . . by which children attribute desirable characteristics to objects which do not possess them' (ibid.: 156). For example, a walking stick could become a horse, inanimate objects could talk, a block could become a house or a church. Adults perpetuated 'the savage state' by writing and reading stories for young children in which animals talked or they had children pretending they were playing a piano, a violin or a drum. Adults could suggest a large brick was a stable and small brick was a horse. Bricks could be rearranged to represent something else. Adults supposed they were developing children's minds by 'making them accept fantastic things as realities', for example, Santa Claus. These were 'the fruits of our imagination' while the children believed them. Their 'credulity is a characteristic of immature minds' (ibid.: 259). She advocated children needed to be normalized. Montessori education was designed to help order the mind. It was about good mental health.

There was no place at all for fantasy for children aged 3–6 years in Montessori education, where the materials were carefully designed to order the child's mind; Montessori explained that it was 'a very common belief that the young child is characterized by a vivid imagination . . . and a special education should be adopted to cultivate this special gift of nature' (Montessori, 1916: 255). Montessori explained that 'if the idea of the universe be presented to the child in the right way, it will do more than arouse interest, it will create in him admiration and wonder. The child's mind will no longer wander, but become fixed and can work' (1973c: 9).

Creativity

To Montessori creativity was 'in reality a composition and no man could say that man creates artistic products out of nothing'. Every man was able 'to create the beautiful with his mind' but only a few could transfer it into reality 'by means of the senses' (Montessori, 1916: 245). Accordingly, she devised sensorial materials precisely to aid and educate the senses to awaken 'creativity [which was] firmly allied to reality' (ibid.: 248). She defined a great artist as one who is 'able to recognise the beautiful in detail . . . possesses the absolute sense of the beautiful . . . and readily perceives any disproportion of form' (ibid.: 338, 339). It was the sensorial materials which aided to refine the senses and help the development of creativity. The creation of art 'is constructed with materials' (ibid.: 245). Montessori described the various materials for creativity in *The Montessori Method* (1964). The children in the first Casa drew with chalks, crayons and coloured pencils, painted with water colours and worked with clay. Professor Randone's exercises for pottery to make vases and bricks were incorporated (Montessori, 1964: 162). The bricks were used to build low walls round the garden plots. Attempts were made by some small children to build small houses. From this, children learned to appreciate objects and constructions in their environment (ibid.: 163, 166). Montessori (1965b) declared 'there can be no graduated exercises in drawing (or painting) leading up to an artistic creation . . . children can be prepared indirectly'. The artist 'perfects himself by refining powers of observation' and by working with sensorial materials. Creation itself is constructed with materials (Montessori, 1965b: 251, 254).

Twenty years later Montessori wrote about the new 'free drawing' in modern schools of advanced ideas but children in Montessori schools 'do not produce of their own accord . . . those dreadful paintings which are displayed and lauded . . . those strange daubs where the child has to explain what he intends to represent by his incomprehensible attempt' (Montessori, 1967b: 284, 285). Montessori children learned indirectly about form and colour and their drawings and paintings were clear and harmonious. Dr Revesz, a psychologist dedicated especially to art, commented, 'the Montessori School does not repress free drawing . . . it makes children find the greatest pleasure in free drawing along with the free development of their sense of colour and form' (ibid.: 288). Children 'compose artistic representations by cutting out coloured paper' like those of Oswald, the famous Viennese physicist (ibid.: 285).

Critics and supporters

The editor of *Communications* reminds us that 'guiding children to the artistic skills and artistic appreciation began in 1912' (Association Montessori Internationale [AMI], 1969: 9). From the 1960s a number of commentators directed their attention to Montessori's educational ideas and creativity, as seen below.

Nancy Rambusch felt that Montessori neglected creativity and added several new activities to the Montessori programme to specially suit American children because recent research showed that children had 'a need for creativity' (Rambusch, 1962: 31).

When Beth Stubbs visited Montessori environments in the United States and England, she observed 'there was an absence of material for dramatic and imaginative play' (Stubbs, 1966: 24). Ada Renwick, an Australian, commented that 'Montessori's materialistic approach had disregard for aesthetic subjects' (Renwick, 1967: 160) while Benjamin Spock deplored the lack of 'hand creative materials' (Frost, 1968: 76).

Deirdre Carr wrote of the many creative activities offered in Montessori schools and gives details of how children can be prepared indirectly for painting, paper work, drawing, printing and modelling (Carr, 1969: 11, 12). Britta Schill believed that children should be given sand, water and paint without rules for using them. To give rules 'is in contradiction to modern theories of child development'. Children should be allowed to experience 'the triumphant experiences of finding out for themselves'. They are deprived of a chance to discover 'the cause and effect relationships between a too-full-brush and drip-on-paper'. Also, children are not given opportunities to use their imaginations and there was no doubt that 'imagination does play an important role in the development of children' (Schill, 1974: 32, 34). A more recent commentator, P. S. Kaplan, believed that in Montessori education there was 'little use of imagination. These activities are not forbidden but they are not encouraged' (Kaplan, 1991: 378).

Anthony Potts concluded that Montessori's contributions to education were 'relatively few' but 'very important'. He stated bluntly, 'Montessori rejected creativity' (Potts, 1980: 41).

Cosmic education (6–12 years) use of imagination

At 6 years, 'if the idea of the universe be presented to the child in the right way, it will do more than arouse interest, it will create in him admiration and wonder'. The child's mind 'will no longer wander, but will become fixed and can work' (Montessori, 1973c: 9). For children aged 6–12 years, the mind 'bases itself on the imagination' at the abstract level and 'has need of support . . . needs to be organized. Only then can the mind attain a higher level . . . penetrating the infinite' (Montessori, 1973c: 38). From the development of the mind, a study outline presented itself, the study of living beings through classification (ibid.: 39).

Classification would help memory and order the mind. Imagination had to be aroused and 'the best way was to present the **whole** with grandeur and mystery' (Montessori, 1975: 37). Children are introduced to the first Great Story 'The Creation of the Universe'. Introducing young children to the universe meant 'all the factors of culture could be introduced but *not in a syllabus* to be imposed on him, nor with the exactitude of detail, but in broadcasting the maximum number of seeds of interest' (Montessori, 1961: 5). Central to Montessori education was that teachers need to follow children's interests.

From 1910, as Montessori continued her observations and experiments, she provided 'answers to children's questions about their world and man's place in it' at 6 years of age through what she called 'The Cosmic Plan' (Montessori, 1975: 1). The new curriculum was decided because there was 'a plan to which the *whole* universe is subject . . . a universal plan' and the child was part of it (ibid.: 1, 2). The Cosmic Plan 'can be presented to the child as a thrilling tale of the earth we live in . . . and who is led through thrilling epochs of world history' (ibid.: 2, 3). Her plan was to bring the world into the classroom. History was to be introduced by 'giving living documented truth using prepared moving films' (Montessori, 1965c: 198). This idea was 'beyond resources', so it was decided that new sets of school books needed to be written and published 'to show complete pictures of reality and factual situations' because none was available (ibid.). Geography was to be introduced through travel stories and Natural Science through stories of insects and other creatures (ibid.: 200). The Universe as a whole would be presented to children 'in an acceptable manner suited to the child's psychology' (ibid.: 19) through 'great stories' which were based on scientific evidence, anthropology and history and were to be continually updated as new information was found. The five great stories:

> The Creation of the Universe (scientific view with all religious views studied)
> The Coming of Life

The Coming of Human Beings
The Story of Communications and Signs
The Story of Numbers

were to be told once every year from the age of 6 years. Children could be stimulated by 'the seeds of interest already sown by attractive literary and pictorial material, all correlated to a central idea of greatly ennobling inspiration' (Montessori 1974: 1) and create in him admiration and wonder (ibid.: 9). The Great Stories were meant to arouse children's imaginations in the creation and development of the Universe. The Big Bang theory was introduced through drama, an exciting experience for the young 6-year-old children, and of deeper significance for the older children who had heard the story before. For them it led to further research. Stories of creation from different religions and cultures were also introduced. At 6 years, imagination had to be aroused and the 'best way was to present "the whole" with grandeur and mystery' (Montessori: 1973: 37). Montessori made it clear that it was possible 'to bring the whole by means of the presentation of detail', first 'through classification', which in turn 'helped understanding and aided memory' (ibid.: 38, 39).

To introduce the idea of 'whole' in nature, by beginning with the planet, could lead to any branch of science for older children's research, including mineralogy, biology, physics, chemistry, with the result that 'examination of detail triggers study as a whole' (ibid.: 40). But it was essential for teachers to understand that 'to teach details (in isolation) is to bring confusion; to establish relationships between things is to bring knowledge' (ibid.: 93, 94). Children 6–12 years have to come to realize that everything in the universe is related to every other thing in the universe, directly or indirectly. Montessori education embraced both 'bottom-up' and 'top-down' approaches to learning.

Critics and supporters

Aline Wolf, a staunch supporter of Montessori education, states, 'Maria Montessori was ahead of her time when she placed cosmic education as the centre piece of her elementary programme . . . she began with the miracle of the cosmos, filling the children with a great sense of awe as one by one they encountered all the wonders of creation that preceded them in history . . . gives the child first an all-encompassing sense of the universe' (Wolf, 1996: 89). Wolf notes that Montessori began her work on Cosmic education 'in the early 1930s' (ibid.: 90).

It was 1960 when Jerome Bruner advocated the 'spiral curriculum' and presented the bold hypothesis 'that any subject can be taught effectively in some intellectually honest form to any child at any stage of development' (Bruner, 1960: 33) because at a later date the same topic would be studied at a more advanced level of development. Mario Montessori Jr challenged this by stating 'the idea was *bold* when Maria Montessori started to experiment with it sixty years ago and startled the world with the obtained results' (Montessori Jr, 1976: 19). Lawrence Stenhouse put forward the notion that 'emergent curriculum must be grounded in classroom practice. The principle sources were the psychology of learning, study of child development, social psychology and sociology of learning' (Stenhouse, 1975: 25). Barry MacDonald and Rob Walker (1976: 4) posed the question, 'Why start with theory, rather than action?'

Montessori had trialled and tested that in 1907.

For Egan (1983), the centrality of stories in the early years was important because story telling always captured the attention of children. Edelsky stresses that teachers 'should be tuned into the interests of students' and curriculum 'should be grounded in students' lives' . . . 'and be partners in creating the menu to be studied'. These sentiments echo Montessori's. But all teachers know there is something about listening to stories that fascinate children (of all ages), and stories continue to remain supreme as a source of language and learning (Mallett, 1999). Children's attention is held because as the story progresses their imagination is actively conjuring up the pictures they create, whether it be truth or fantasy. Montessori used imagination based on truth so the mind developed normally.

Montessori, the Teacher and the Prepared Environment

Chapter outline

The prepared environment: a plan for allowing children to develop according to natural laws.

(Montessori, 1964; 1961: 81)

Providing the correct environment was apparent to Montessori in the first Casa dei Bambini in 1907 where she studied non-deficient children in a scientific manner (Montessori, 1964: 42, 43). Over many years she stressed the importance of the prepared environment and how it was designed to permit the psychological development of each child (Montessori, 1965c: 65). She reminded teachers at every opportunity that 'preparing the environment for normal, healthy development is difficult' but it was needed for all stages of development (Montessori, 1974: 97). She noted that a special environment had been created for living, within the first Casa (Montessori, 1978: 202), where children lived and worked together harmoniously as a community. It was twice the size of a normal classroom (Montessori, 1965c: 112) with high ceilings and large windows for light and ventilation. There were detailed specifications to be considered. Each *prepared environment* 'is to have only one set of each type of material' (Montessori lecture, India, 1942) because 'one piece of each material enables the child to reduce his mind to order' (Montessori, 1961: 124). There were to be just enough materials to satisfy children's love of activity by containing objects which children 'can move, use and put back. The attraction of such surroundings is inexhaustible' (ibid.: 123).

The first impressions to strike you when entering a Montessori environment should be the orderliness, the spotless, hygienically clean attractiveness of the furnishings. It was to be inviting, enticing, enchanting. The beautiful room has bare floors, a few tables and chairs of different sizes set out to accommodate children of different ages. Small mats define work areas on the floor. Uncluttered low shelves display the materials within easy reach of children. Everything is in soft pleasing colours and Montessori materials are made of natural woods. All have a calming effect on children, rather than bright colours which over stimulate children. There are no objects to distract children's attention. No mobiles, no displays of art work, no distractions at all. Montessori suggested only one painting, Raphael's Madonna della Seggiola, which signifies motherhood.

By 1910, when Montessori began to plan for elementary education, there were many new materials to be designed for children aged 6–12 years. These included new materials for practical life while all other subject areas had special hands-on materials for language, mathematics (including an introduction to algebra and geometry) and cultural subjects – history, geography, science, natural science, art and music. It was a wide curriculum designed for integrated studies. Later in the 1930s when Cosmic education was introduced many more new materials were introduced enabling children to learn how everything was interrelated.

Critics and supporters

Aspects of a prepared environment

In the late 1950s, Nancy Rambusch, a supporter of Montessori education and one who has been acknowledged for reintroducing Montessori education to the United States, was reported as saying that members of the American Nursery Schools 'believed it was artificial to prepare the environment in advance' (Rambusch, 1962: 26). For A. M. Gillet, the prepared environment, the result of years of scientific observations, 'was necessary for the formation of children's intelligence' (Gillet, 1969: 69). James McVicker Hunt reminded readers that 'the prepared environment was set up for experimental purposes and the issue was, 'Which environment was best to produce the correct result?' (Hunt, 1974: 147). The result being, an adult who could contribute to society.

More recent commentators, Blenkin and Kelly, advocates of 'education as development', note that 'one of the most neglected aspects of school is the creation of an environment and those who teach older children consider the classroom environment is of no importance at all (Blenkin and Kelly, 1996: 1). There are four key factors in creating an environment, according to Wood (1994), and these are physical features, materials, organization and climate. The climate in the classroom should be relaxed where children feel secure, can interact easily with each other and staff (McClay, 1996). For Cambourne (1984) and Gee (1996) the importance of the environment is crucial because it leads to the construction of a humane, just society in which children can engender useful ideas. For Lankshear et al. (1997) the environment should be 'enchanting'. Since 1907 Montessori environments have met these criteria.

There were responses about the new Montessori materials. A scathing comment from T. Raymont in 1937 was that 'the didactic material is characteristic of a Doctor's prescription and nothing can take its place' (Raymont, 1937: 309). Margaret Drummond who trained under Montessori praised 'learning by experiment and thought' (Drummond, 1947: 8). She experimented herself and produced valuable materials for mathematics for children 5–12 years.

Beth Stubbs claimed that Australian preschools had materials 'richer in variety' than those offered by Montessori education (Stubbs, 1966: 25). A. M. Gillet expressed concern that experienced Montessori teachers kept adding material to Montessori material which showed every single step and feared that 'this excessive increase of material would lead to sclerosis of the intelligence . . . and kill the child's sense of observation and imagination'. She reminded the audience of Montessori's recommendation 'to keep the material limited', because material stimulated the imagination, while too much material hindered the development of the imagination. A child's intelligence is seen in the ways different materials are used and compared. Development of the senses allows observations of the relationships between materials which leads to discoveries being made both inside and outside the classroom. This is the beginning of consciousness that everything in the world is interrelated. (Gillet, Montessori Conference, Bergamo, Italy, 1969). Emmy Louise Wider was under the impression that 'experimentation, exploration amid improvisation with materials was NOT permitted' (Wider, 1970: 57). In 1976, Beryl Edmonds visited a Montessori environment in the Northern Territory, Australia, and noted 'there is not enough material and its use is too limiting for the child's resourcefulness' (Edmonds, 1976: 3).

Mario Montessori announced that research continued 'with the preparation and production of eventually *new* Montessori material' (Grazzini, 1975: 17). These materials are now available and many are for geometry and algebra. Montessori materials were being produced years after Montessori's death. Montessori noted that she had made 'a great variety of didactic materials . . . I have never seen a complete set in any institution' (Montessori, 1964: 36).

Implications for research

Susan Isaacs, a staunch Montessori supporter, 'had a profound influence, direct and indirect, on the development of informal education in England' (Silberman, 1973: 179). She began an experimental school, using a Montessori environment in *The Malting House*, for young children in Cambridge in 1920 where Montessori visited and lectured. Susan Isaacs recorded her observations which formed the basis of much of her writings on learning and child development by which 'she influenced a whole generation of teachers, head teachers, inspectors, educationists and educational researchers'. To her 'the children . . . are the living aim' (ibid.). She became the first chairperson of the Child Development Department of The University of London Institute of Education. It was after World War II that Sir Alec Clegg, 'widely acknowledged as one of the greats of British education', and Susan Isaacs were involved in 'the quiet revolution' which transformed British education (ibid.: 65). Susan Isaacs died in 1948. Several years later, Nancy Rambusch completed her Montessori Training at St Nicholas Montessori College in London. She visited many English Infant schools before her return to the United States where she opened her famous Montessori school at Newport in the mid-1950s. Lilian Weber, Professor of Early Childhood Education at New York's City College, travelled to England in 1966 because 'I discovered that England had what I considered to be "good" education, even with large classes' (Weber, 1971: 63). She enrolled at the University of London Institute of Education, visited 56 schools over a period of 18 months and finished 'an exhaustive analysis' of these schools which was published as a book *The English Infant School and Informal Education* (Weber, 1971: 62–6). Nancy Rambusch was working at the same New York College at that time and later became Professor of Early Childhood Education. It was not until the Plowden Report in 1967 that the changes which had taken place in English education came to light. And so, it was to England that 'American educators mainly turned for examples of what open education can be' (ibid.: 5). The underlying assumption of informal schools, both British and American, is that 'in an enriched and carefully planned *environment* that supports the natural drive of learning, children are mostly able to learn by themselves, from each other and from books' (Schneir and Schneir, 1971: 30). It has to be 'an *environment* bursting with invitation' (Weber, 1971: 64), and a Montessori environment does that.

The Montessori directress

The teacher must be transformed.

(Montessori, 1965b: 111)

The directress was considered by Montessori as part of the environment. The role of the directress, a new model of teacher, evolved over a long period of experimentation and it became complex. As the living component within the environment, the first requirement of the directress was to prepare herself spiritually through self-analysis and cater for the spiritual needs of the children by maintaining a classroom climate where children could become 'happy, confident and loving masters of the house' (Montessori, 1964: 348). With a deep interest in the spiritual (mental) development and social development of children, she was to direct them in their daily lives, to remain calm at all times, to have peace of mind and to be 'passive much more than active' (ibid.: 87). She was also to change children's tasks in school 'from drudgery to joy' (Montessori, 1973c: 1). Her priority was to understand child development, and her fundamental task was to help development. Montessori was convinced that 'to be able to help life we must be able to understand the laws that govern it. We need an education based on the care of the living' (Montessori, 1967a: 12). The directress was to put Montessori principles into practice all of which were based on the natural tendencies of children which Montessori had observed in 1907. Over the years, Montessori described the role of directress as encompassing a number of different aspects.

A valet – to serve the spirit

The fundamental function of the directress was to have 'techniques analogous to those of a valet; they are to serve, and serve well: to serve the spirit' (Montessori, 1967a: 281). To serve the spirit, she was required to remain patient, calm, dignified, tolerant, self-controlled, non-judgemental and humble all the while learning from the child. She catered for the spiritual needs of the children by maintaining a classroom climate where children could be happy, confident and loving. She prepared herself spiritually, and instead of being proud and claiming to be infallible, 'she assumes the vesture of humility' (Montessori, 1965c: 100) realizing children taught themselves and recognizing that she was successful when 'free children are working as though I do not exist' (Montessori, 1967a: 283). She understood that the spirit of the child could be nurtured by allowing him to explore and experiment with the materials, making discoveries through trial and error and being a successful learner. She had no ambitions for herself, her spiritual happiness deriving from helping each student reach his potential (Montessori, 1974: 89).

A custodian of the environment

As classroom custodian yet 'an unobtrusive part of the environment' (Montessori, 1973: 39), each directress prepared and maintained the environment, with all materials meticulously in order, in beautiful, shining, perfect condition. There, the active, exuberant learners were to experience physical, psychological and spiritual freedom. She was to help the development of the whole child to enable each child develop his personality by keeping in mind the basic principle of Montessori education which was 'the liberty of pupils in their spontaneous manifestations' (Montessori, 1964: 80). The appearance of the directress was the first step in gaining a child's confidence and respect; it was desirable that she should possess excellent speech standards, grace in movements, unfailing courtesy and a sensitive, sympathetic nature. Forty years later these attributes were substantially unchanged: the directress should be preferably young, charmingly dressed, scented with cleanliness, happy and graciously dignified (Montessori, 1973c: 87), all of which helped to nurture the spirit of the child.

A facilitator of learning

As 'the facilitator of the child's learning' she acted as the *trait d'union* between the materials and the child (Montessori, 1975: 39), and because she understood child development, she judged the appropriate time to introduce a new piece of material to a child, and she knew through her teacher preparation how to introduce the material by exact demonstration to each child. The principle which brought success to the directress was this: 'as soon as concentration has begun, act as if the child does not exist' (Montessori, 1973c: 87). The advice to the directresses in the first Casa was 'our duty to the child was to give a ray of light and go on our way' (Montessori, 1964: 115). To be successful using the materials was extremely important to the child because 'the material is the base from which the spirit soars' and 'the staircase for the student to ascend' (Montessori, 1965c) to a higher plane of development. The directress supported each child 'by standing behind him and allowing him to go forward as far as he can' which was very different to the general teaching method of 'standing in front of the child and preventing him from going further than the limits imposed on him by the teacher' (Montessori, 1973c: 65) who followed a syllabus.

A caretaker of children

As caretaker of the children, the directress provided a stress-free environment and helped to nurture each child's development (Montessori, 1967a: 252) because of her knowledge of the absorbent mind and sensitive periods. Further observations by Montessori revealed that 'nature lays down a plan for construction both of personality and social life' (ibid.: 133). Social development and emotional development evolve together and are helped by the congenial, social conditions provided by the directress.

An observant scientist

As 'scientist and skilled observer', the directress witnessed 'children working with materials in silent fascination' (Montessori, 1967a: 252). She must be 'a lover of nature (the child)' (Montessori, 1964: 104) and prepare herself spiritually through self-analysis, eradicating obstacles from the environment which impede children's development and be willing to accept guidance and be taught by the children and others (Montessori, 1978: 149). As an objective observer she was to give a large proportion of her life to her work as she discovered cures for any deviations in the behaviour of children in her care. She would carefully observe children making discoveries for themselves and be totally open-minded, non-prejudicial, inquiring and humble (Montessori, 1965c: 131).

> When I am in the midst of children I do not think of myself as a scientist, a theoretician. When I am with children I am a nobody . . . this enables me to see things one would miss if one was a somebody, little thing, simple but very precious truths.
>
> (Montessori, 1967b: 101)

A researcher

As 'a researcher' there were important factors to be observed in the study of each individual child over a period of time. Notes were made of the materials selected and how long the child worked with them, individual differences, development of abstraction, stages of intellectual development, and the acquisition of self-discipline, normalization and independence were recorded objectively. Character development was observed and attributed to nature or nurture (Montessori, 1965c: 87–9). The directress knew where each child 'was' developmentally (Montessori, 1978: 150). Every individualized three-period lesson gave her an opportunity to be a researcher. She received immediate feedback as to whether the child had understood the lesson or not by observing how the child worked and explored using the materials.

Preparing the environment

The duty of a directress was to prepare the environment. There are five distinct areas to be set out and can be clearly recognized in any Montessori environment:

Practical life to develop the child's sense of order, coordination and independence through daily life activities, including social graces and courtesy.

Sensorial education to enable the refinement of each child's five senses through activities and to broaden their understanding of the environment and the world.

Language to increase the child's receptive and expressive language ability through auditory, visual and cognitive experiences and activities. To prepare the hand for writing and so enable the child to compose and read with understanding. After 1910 Montessori made many more materials for the elementary children and when she updated *The Montessori Method* (1964) in *The Discovery of the Child* (1967b) she describes how many pieces designed for older children were used with the younger children. For English speaking children, extra spelling and reading materials were needed for the non-phonetic words.

Mathematics to enable the child to have full understanding of the mathematical processes as opposed to memorizing operations or facts through rote learning. Many new pieces of materials for mathematics, algebra and geometry were developed, and, again, many found their way into Cycle 1, because the young children, it was discovered, could understand and complete operations for addition, subtraction, multiplication and division to 9999 using golden bead materials, could build a binomial cube and a trinomial cube (algebra) and the geometric cabinet offered a variety of geometric plane figures.

Culture to offer the child experiences in geography, history, art, art history, biology, zoology, botany, music, music appreciation and creative arts all using concrete materials first before moving towards the abstract (Montessori, 1965b; 1967b). Many interesting materials for every subject are available today.

These five learning areas are found in every Montessori environment.

Putting principles into practice

Montessori found that directresses 'understood the principles of the method but have difficulty in putting it into practice' (Montessori, 1964: 87). Those difficulties included:

- Having large blocks of uninterrupted time for the children to follow their individual interests and three-hour blocks of time are common in Montessori schools. (Montessori, 1967a)
- Teaching 'becomes easier since we do not need to choose what we shall teach'. (Montessori, 1946b: 5)
- Allowing each child to choose, anything of interest from the wide curriculum which now included Cosmic education. The directress 'has to satisfy children's mental hunger, unlike a non-Montessori teacher who is limited by the syllabus – prescribing just so much of every subject to be imparted within a set time'. (Montessori, 1974: 8)
- Having no set plan for the day's work nor following a timetable but '*following the child*', a form of respect, 'and helping him which is the task of the educator'. (Montessori, 1961: 103)

It was from Itard that Montessori took the directive 'Follow the child', and from 1898 there has been one method in Montessori from birth to adulthood – follow the psychic needs of the child. Peterson (1992) suggested that teachers 'Follow the child' because 'when I join their march – the programme goes where they are going'. He urges teachers 'to try to take the child's lead' (in Edelsky, 1999: 118, 150) without an explanation of how this was to be achieved. Montessori demonstrated how individual teaching was possible with more than 40 children and one directress.

Multi-age grouping

In 1907, Montessori found herself with a group of multi-aged children who were in the same developmental period spanning 3 years which she saw as an advantage and commented: 'We have little ones of two and a half who cannot as yet make sense of the sensorial exercises and children of five and a half who because of their development might easily pass into third elementary' (Montessori, 1964: 373). A number of significant observations were made by Montessori over 30 years about the advantage of multi-age grouping, including the following:

- Tasks were matched to each child's stage of development.
- A fast developer was extended but still worked alongside peers.
- A slow developer never felt he could not achieve because his task matched his needs.
- Socially, multi-age grouping allowed the young to 'emulate the old, and the old can teach the young' and sometimes 'there are things a teacher cannot convey to a child of three but a child of five can do it with utmost ease'.
- 'Segregation by age, unlike vertical grouping, is a fundamental mistake which breeds a host of evils.'
- 'Reciprocal helpfulness' in the multi-age class 'gets cemented by affection' (Montessori, 1939: 205–6).
- The change from a class to a society through social cohesion with classes of 40 or more children occurred when a child did not put himself first but rather 'puts the group first' (ibid.: 213).

- The society of mixed aged children 'added charm' to social life 'because of the number of different types one meets'. (ibid.)
- Opportunities for peer/cross-age tutoring were rewarding and enjoyable experiences for children. (ibid.)
- Social experiences within Montessori environments were extremely important for daily living because students live in an active community (ibid.: 226).
- Children learned from each other; the older children were happy to share what they knew, living in harmony without inferiority complexes. (ibid.)
- It became habitual to be polite, to wait one's turn and to solve social problems themselves during every day of school life (ibid.: 227).
- Free children operated with the help of others. There was no envy amongst them because there was no competition for marks or prizes and as a result they admired those who did better than they did. These were natural developments in children when 'rivalry, emulation and ambition were not encouraged' (ibid.: 242).
- Normalized children 'unaided can construct an orderly society' within the classroom and 'solve problems eacefully' (ibid.: 258).
- Vertical groupings in 3-year spans were found in every Montessori environment (ibid.).

In a Montessori environment children were free to discipline each other. This occurred if a child did not respect another child's space or when a child interrupted another child's work. A child could ring a small bell which brought complete silence and then announce that noise was interfering with his work and asks politely, 'Could we have whispering?' Peer intervention was effective because of the feeling of equality and understanding while teacher intervention was not taken in the same light. Well adjusted (normalized) children lived harmoniously together.

After years of experiments, Montessori concluded that the role of the directress was complex. The role of teachers in today's mainstream classrooms is also seen to be complex.

Managing multi-age grouping

There is nothing in Montessori education to tell a directress how to teach or what to teach; she is asked to follow the child, observe the child and present the materials exactly to each child individually in silence or by using a three-period lesson.

To put Montessori principles into practice meant:

- challenging for the directress 'in knowing how to meet unexpected claims on the part of her pupils, of having to teach *then and there* things she had never intended to teach (Montessori, 1961: 41) because each child can choose anything of interest from the wide curriculum.

Directresses must understand the needs of children at each stage of development and should provide every opportunity and time for each child to be a successful, happy learner.

Social and emotional relationships

Traditional relationships between teacher and children in school presumed the teacher's 'superiority, tyranny and domination' which was incorrectly presumed the natural right of the teacher over the child. As a result, the children resisted which was 'a vital defence of his own psychic integrity or an unconscious reaction to oppression' (Montessori, 1978: 152). Montessori called for change because she saw learning as being both *biological and social* (Montessori, 1964). The relationship between teacher and child in a Montessori environment was very different to that in traditional schools. The new directress relinquished her power by not forcing her will on children and by not selecting everything to be done. Instead, she helped the development of personality while 'respecting the interior construction of personality done by the child' (Montessori, 1973: 113) and empowering him to choose his own experiences and to think and act for himself (Montessori, 1967a: 257) in a prepared environment. Each child followed his own agenda as there was no set curriculum or timetable to follow, and it was each child who knew what he needed to help his development, 'to construct himself' (ibid.: 223), and he was better able to choose the material to match that need. Such 'awareness of one's needs and ability to act on them is part of being an autonomous individual' (Montessori, 1965c: 71). The primary purpose of a directress was to help the young child become independent, self-reliant and master of his own destiny epitomised in the words of a child: 'Help me to help myself.'

The directress provided a stress-free environment, with correct social conditions for the development of the whole child, and a climate where 'repression was avoided' (Montessori, 1948b). She did not make corrections in books as this had 'a lowering' effect on children and resulted in losing interest in what they were doing. Also children became discouraged when scolded or insulted as this humiliated or offended them. All of this affected the quality of social life, especially the relationship between the teacher and student. Good relationships were essential in education. There was to be respect and trust between students and directress (Montessori, 1964: 13), along with relationships between student and student (Montessori, 1973c: 89). A directress had 'to possess "great respect" for the *interior* construction of personality' done by the child as it was of 'greatest importance and must be observed in practice' (Montessori, 1975: 111, 112, 113).

In a Montessori environment, free children cooperated with and helped others; there was no envy among them because there was no competition, and as a result they admired those who did better than they did. These were natural developments in children when 'rivalry, emulation and ambition were not encouraged' (Montessori, 1967a: 242). As a result of 'reciprocal helpfulness' the class 'gets cemented by affection' (ibid.: 206). The change from a class to a society through cohesion occurs, when a child does not put himself first but rather 'puts the group first' (ibid.: 213). Further observations revealed that 'nature lays down a plan for construction both of personality and social life' (ibid.: 133).

Children grew to know each other and there was trust and respect between the students and the directress. This was partly due to the short three-period lessons which allowed the directress the opportunity to work with each child every day. Anyone who chose to become a directress had to grasp first the need to empower children. From 3 years, children were to be encouraged and helped to think and act for themselves.

Social development and emotional development evolve together in Montessori education through the social conditions provided and the social relationships between the directress and students. Love was the most powerful emotion, Montessori averred. There were different levels of love. The first was the personal care and affection of a parent; the second was not personal, not material, but was a spiritual relationship practised by the directress (Montessori, 1967a: 283). Love united children and adults and this love 'exists potentially between man and man'. It was universal (Montessori, 1964: 13; 1967a: 289). Montessori observed the universal love for children unified adults, as a result, it was children who could bring peace to the world (Montessori in Geneva, 1932).

Critics and supporters

There were many critics who claimed Montessori 'made no emotional provision in her approach to education and emotions are an important part of self-awareness' (Rambusch, 1962: 28). Nancy Rambusch also pointed out that in Montessori education 'social development and emotional development were the same as cognitive development since they were part of a whole' (ibid.). Montessori did consider that the child's whole personality could not be divided (Montessori, 1967a: 203), but as she had provided the correct living conditions for development in the prepared environment where children became normalized, she had at the same time, provided for social and emotional development.

Work/play

Among the others was Evelyn Beyer who averred that Montessori had not considered feelings and this was 'a lack of awareness of the importance to young children of being able to act out strong feelings of fear, anxiety, anger and delight' (Beyer, 1962: 57). According to Britta Schill 'modern psychology and child psychology have taught us the importance of emotional well-being' (Schill, 1963: 33). Many psychologists, including Evelyn Pitcher, agreed that through play children could work out their frustrations, master their 'fears, angers and jealousies', and that play provides 'wholesome emotional development' (Frost, 1968: 76, 95). For children experiencing frustration, commentators and psychologists saw 'play' as being the answer because it provided children with social experiences in school. Then, Emmy L. Wider drew attention to the fact that 'play was not part of Montessori's system' (Wider, 1970: 57).

Montessori maintained that children did not play, they worked to perfect themselves. She stated 'psychologists say that the child must play, for through play he brings perfection to himself . . . (they) do not help but abandon him to his own devices . . . in such a complicated world how can a child absorb culture if left to play with toys and sand castles?' (Montessori, 1974: 111). Montessori recognized that play was a natural characteristic but 'the aim of play or the activity involved in it is the play or activity itself, and nothing beyond' and what educators 'have to emphasise is nature's plan in implanting the love of play in a child to aid the child's development'. To do this 'we bring the play activities of the child close to reality' (ibid.: 112, 113) in practical life exercises.

The three-period lesson

The three-period lesson was a short, exact demonstration of a piece of didactic material. There was interaction between the directress and the child before the child was left to work with the material for as long as he wished. The child was viewed as an active learner. This aspect of the Montessori Method attracted comment.

Beryl Edmonds argued 'that by showing a child how to use the materials the teacher is imposing the method and "teaching him"' (Edmonds, 1976: 4) when Montessori claimed children 'taught themselves'.

The three-period lesson did resemble Vygotsky's theory, published in Russia in the 1930s, which is often interpreted to be *what a child can do today with help he will be able to do alone tomorrow.* These words carry the same meaning to those used by a Montessori child who said 'help me to do it myself' which became a slogan in Montessori education. Vygotsky (1978) suggested that learning was related to the social relationships between the learner and the teacher, and as a result, the child moved towards a higher plane of development. Montessori saw the social relationship between the directress and the child to be crucial for learning. Both Montessori and Vygotsky stressed that learning was done by the active learners and not by teaching. Every three-period lesson was designed to allow observation of natural development. Careful and detailed anecdotal notes were made of how the materials were used but the real development was *inner.*

Assessment

Continuous evaluation with anecdotal and qualitative notes were made of each child. *Statistics* were not kept. Montessori could not see that a number could measure a child's development. She noted 'Assessment of *bad marks* with which teachers weigh up the work of girls and boys is like measuring lifeless objects with a balance'. Their work 'is measured like inanimate matter, not judged as a product of life' (Montessori, 1975: 100). *Each child was a case study.*

In 1971, Evans reported that it 'was becoming increasingly apparent that a child's learning could not be determined wholly by his 'mental age' but can be assessed more accurately from a determination of sensory development (Evans, 1971: 63).

In the early 1970s when Charles Silberman, like hundreds of fellow American *educators*, visited England to observe Open Classrooms, asked Sir Alec Clegg if he had *statistics* to show the achievements of students in 'informal' schools. This showed evidence that schools in the United States were still using IQ tests, classroom tests and examinations. Sir Alec produced a folio of samples of children's work and added 'all these are by-products: *the children are the products*' (Silberman, 1973: 65). He confirmed that there were no intelligence test results, no reading techniques and no history syllabus to show, but it was the way children took part day to day in the classroom and 'how they behave towards one another that was important' (ibid.). It sounded very much like a Montessori answer from the time she began her work in the Casa dei Bambini in 1907. But then, it was the English infant schools in which Susan Isaacs, a student of Montessori, had so much influence.

Vertical grouping

Ada Renwick was concerned about extension work for the 'bright' child when she wrote that 'the modern teacher may feel that Montessori provides little opportunity for extending the "bright" child' (Renwick, 1967: 155). If bright meant a fast developer, not a deviation, then Ada Renwick was mistaken. In a multi-age classroom, the bright child was allowed to go forward and work was matched to each child's stage of development, but he still worked along with his peers. Also, a slow developer never felt he could not achieve because his task satisfied his needs. Children did not compete for stars, marks or prizes, and as Montessori observed 'children of different ages helped each other' (Montessori, 1967a: 206). A benefit of vertical grouping led the group to solidarity with a responsibility towards each other.

Implications for education

To become a Montessori teacher called for change from the 'traditional' teacher. Changes to make include:

- love, respect and trust each child
- become an unobtrusive observer of child development
- know the stage of development of each child
- be calm and inhibit own personality when children are working

- be able to present three-period lessons
- be able to present all Montessori materials
- keep all other lessons brief
- empower every child to choose and plan his work
- follow each child's interests
- be prepared to teach anything that occurs incidentally
- learn not to interrupt, or praise when not necessary
- keep the environment beautiful with every piece of material intact
- be patient with deviant children knowing they will become normalized
- be just by helping each child to reach his potential
- reflect with the purpose of improving your skills
- manage the class according to Montessori principles
- create a happy, stress-free living environment.

Social relationships today

Today students in schools are still assessed by marks, homework and examinations. Relationships between teachers and students have become more strained than ever because a high percentage of marks depend on internal school assessment. Many students fear that their assessment is based on relationship with the teacher rather than academic achievement. It was not until 1978 that the work of Lev Vygotsky (1896–1939), a Russian psychologist, was published in English. His sociocultural theory suggested that learning was related to the relationship between the student and the teacher (Vygotsky, 1978; Wertsch, 1985). It could be possible that Vygotsky was aware also of Montessori's writing because *The Montessori Method* was translated into Russian in 1912, and a Montessori classroom was set up that year in the Tsar's palace in St Petersburg for the royal children. In his work with language, Vygotsky noted, 'many words in part have the same meaning for the child and the adult, especially words referring to concrete objects . . . *"meanings meet"* in the same concrete object, and this suffices to ensure mutual understanding' (Vygotsky: 1986: 110). Lohmann pointed out that it was 'the meeting of the child and adult minds' which Vygotsky referred to as 'the zone of proximal development' (Lohmann, 1988: 18). The zone of proximal development (ZPD) was defined as 'the distance between the actual developmental level and the level of potential development as determined through problem solving under adult supervision or collaboration with more capable peers' (Vygotsky, 1986: 111; Wertsch, 1985: 8). Those who know Montessori education and the three-period lesson can see correlations between Vygotsky and Montessori. Vygotsky pointed out that 'we know too little about how to define or pinpoint a child's "zone of development" . . . but it is useful in telling us what we cannot know about children' (Lohmann, 1988: 19). Montessori wrote much about *what we can never really know about a child*. It was only the child who knew exactly the stage of development he had reached and that is why *he knew best* what to choose to satisfy his needs for his psychic development at any given time (Montessori, Lecture 1/1 London, c. 1930). This was the child's *secret* which he never revealed and should not be questioned about it. The child should be allowed *to keep his secret*.

Montessori, Parents and the Home Environment 6

Home, school and society must combine in the education of the child.

(Montessori, 1967a: 13)

In Montessori educational philosophy, parents play an important role. When the first Casa dei Bambini in the San Lorenzo Quarter of Rome opened in 1907, Montessori was aware that Senor Edouard Tamalo, the owner of the large tenement building, wished all the preschool aged children, between the age of 3 and 7 years, to attend. When these children had been left alone and unsupervised by their working parents during the long working day, they were destroying his investment. A schoolroom for these children would solve his problem. The successful results of the first Casa dei Bambini became widely known, and soon another classroom was opened in the same district. At the Inaugural Address of the second Casa dei Bambini,

Montessori expressed the advantages of such an environment for young children. She spoke of 'the union of the family and the school in the matter of educational aims' and how in state schools 'the family is always something far away from the school . . . regarded as rebelling against their ideals' (Montessori, 1964: 63).

From the very beginning Montessori parents were to have a role in their children's education. Part of the rent paid by parents went towards the maintenance of the apartment used by the children. The idea of 'collective ownership of the school is new and very beautiful and profoundly educational' (ibid.). Now, 'mothers could leave their little ones in a place, not only safe, but where they had every advantage . . . and go away to work with easy minds'. Montessori told the assembled group that 'until the present time only one class in society might have this advantage . . . *rich* mothers'. Not only did Montessori emancipate the children and the teacher, she emancipated the mothers. She had already represented the women of Italy when she addressed the Feminist Congress in Berlin in 1896, the year she graduated from the University of Rome (Montessori, 1964) and again at the Feminist Congress in London in 1900 (Kramer, 1976). She fought tirelessly for social justice and rights for women as well as children.

Mothers of children attending the first Casa were invited 'to go at any hour of the day to watch, to admire or to meditate upon the life in the Casa' (ibid.: 64, 65). Later, Montessori was to restrict the visits to the classroom, but she was available to parents daily to discuss any matters relating to the welfare of their children. She gave free advice on medical, dietary and scholastic matters. The work in the classroom was a true social venture. She had many requests from parents wherever a Casa opened and within a very short period Case dei Bambini were opened for all classes of children in many parts of the world.

A main principle of Montessori education was the matter of *the union of the family and the school* (Montessori, 1964: 63). She announced in 1907 that parent education was to be part of Montessori education. *Dr Montessori's Own Handbook*, first published in 1914, was written to help parents understand Montessori principles and methods. A main aim of Montessori education was to improve the living conditions of children. The problem of improving living conditions remains today for many children worldwide as they continue to experience very poor living conditions within classrooms and at home.

Montessori explained to parents in her *Own Handbook:*

> The importance of Montessori education lay in the effects which it produces in children. It is the child who proves the value of this method by his spontaneous magnifications, which seem to reveal the laws of man's inner development.
>
> (Montessori, 1965b: 182)

Parents were asked to complement the Montessori classroom by implementing the principles *not* by duplicating and working with materials. No set homework was given and so spared stressed relationships between home and school. 'Mothers and fathers must shoulder their responsibilities together' (Montessori, 1967a: 13), and there were so many ways in which a child could be helped to do things for himself at home. He could learn to care for many of his own needs and become independent of adults from a young age if he was shown how. He needed to be shown how to bathe and dry himself, brush and comb his hair, dress and undress, blow his nose, learn to be toilet trained and wash his hands as early as he was able to do so. Also, some time was needed at meal time on how to hold and use cutlery properly so he could feed himself. Some children would need to be shown several times and help was given, but only if required. It was stressed that anything a child could do himself, he should be allowed time to do. As part of the family, the toddler learned to help with simple chores, care for a pet and help in the garden. There were daily routines and cleaning jobs to be done. He learned to be cooperative and was always given things to do that he could do successfully and made him feel he contributed to family life. He was to be helped to develop a good work ethic so that later he helped to keep the house tidy doing daily chores. Good manners and graciousness were to be demonstrated by older members of the family so that politeness became inherent. Parents were to be reliable, keep promises, tell the truth, be available to help the child but to let the child do things he could do for himself. Children have always needed to feel secure and be able to trust those they love. Families can do interesting things together following their children's interests as well as their own. Each child is encouraged to think for himself and to ask questions. In this way adults can assist the child's development, satisfy his curiosity, his eagerness to know. An independent child who can contribute, feels he is part of the family, is a happy child.

A topic Montessori often discussed with parents was that the adult had to slow down and work at a child's rate. For example, to go for as walk at a child's pace. Simply, the adult had to learn to see things from a child's point of view and 'follow the child' which meant they had to learn about how children developed.

Understanding child development

Montessori explained to parents how from birth the child's absorbent mind is like a camera. The newborn focuses and absorbs everything in the room at a glance (like the click of a camera) and the information that is processed and developed cannot be observed (like the development of a photograph). The infant's absorbent mind processes and develops language in the same manner, unseen by the observer (Montessori, 1965b).

It was useful for mothers to understand that there are developmental stages of obedience. Will power and obedience develop hand in hand and adults should help develop the will not break the will. Before 3 years, a child cannot obey because he lacks understanding. Conscious will power has to be helped and cultivated, but not broken. At 2 years, many children have tantrums because they cannot communicate and are misunderstood. Montessori suggests that parents should give in to the child and not demand obedience because there are three stages of obedience. Montessori explains:

1) The child obeys sometimes but not always. If the request corresponds to one of his vital urges he will obey. Will not developed sufficiently.
2) Can obey but not always because he is still not in complete control of his will.
3) Can obey and does always giving up what he is doing willingly (type of love).

(Montessori, 1967a: 256–61)

Older children who are vocal can be given reasons for acceptable behaviour and obedience, but care has to be taken that it is a discussion, not an argument. Children sometimes need help to understand they are to be masters of themselves and their environment but not masters of the adults who care for them.

The silence game offers an opportunity to test will power (ibid.). We must help the child to act for himself, will for himself, think for himself. This is the act of those who aspire to serve the spirit (life of the mind) (Montessori, 1974: 89). Silence is golden, good for the spirit and needs to be experienced daily in life.

At the International Montessori Congress, London, 1951, which Montessori attended, Miss E. M. Thorn, a nurse addressed the group on *Montessori in the Home* where, she pointed out, 'there were many opportunities for a toddler to exercise and develop his will. One was being allowed to choose what he would do, because to be able to make correct choices was one of the most important of life's skills and needed to be practised from the earliest age'.

Mental health

Montessori referred parents to the new psychology in education by explaining that each Children's House 'is a laboratory . . . the essential factor in psychological research, especially in the research of psychogenesis, the origin and development of the mind, must be established of normal conditions for the free development of thought' (Montessori, 1965b: 182). She assured parents that children were given 'the right means of development' and that through liberty 'children's rebellion has no more reason for existence . . . resulting in a series of outbursts of joy' in the classroom (ibid.: 184). Parents and children at this time were not familiar with children being happy at school.

Fantasy

Montessori often spoke to parent groups about fantasy and aimless play activities as being a danger to the development of a child's mind. Parents were reminded they were to help not hinder development. Aimless play was bad for any child's mental health and mental health was the priority of Montessori's work. She constantly reminded adults that the mind should be connected with reality which was 'the fundamental basis of mental health and mental development' (Montessori, 1975: 88).

Always being truthful was essential for trust to grow in all relationships but especially so with young children. To Montessori, the study of nature had more fantastic and beautiful 'things' than anyone could make up. Imagination was to be used for imagining real objects or for visualizing useful inventions in the mind. Parents were advised to tell the truth always and not have children believe in fanciful creatures or people, for example, Superman or Santa Claus. Make believe was a danger to mental health and should not be encouraged. Children are credulous and believe parents tell the truth always. Good relationships are based on truth.

Prizes and punishments

Another topic Montessori addressed many times was the principle of 'no prizes and no punishments'. Parents like teachers were to look for signs of the development of each child's inner praise and self-development. Montessori pointed out that 'if a child has to be rewarded or punished, it means he lacks the capacity to guide himself' (Montessori, 1967a: 245). In Alfie Kohn's book *Rewards : The Trouble with Gold Stars* (1993) it is shown that parents, teachers and managers manipulate others with incentives such as 'Do this and you will get that.' It shows evidence from hundreds of studies that in the long run incentives fail and people actually do inferior work. He does not mention Maria Montessori and her thoughts of inner motivation 90 years before.

In the home

The newborn

Montessori pointed out that the child's helper in early infancy 'has a noble task which is to begin to collaborate in the mental development and the formation of character' (Montessori, 1967a: 124) and be supportive and sensitive to the child's needs. She realized that mothers needed help to understand how children develop from the time of birth. As early as 1913 it was reported that she was lecturing, writing and giving advice to mothers about the care of newborns. She averred that the newborn child was not understood by parents and they did not provide for the psychic life of the child from birth, only the physical care (Montessori, 1978: 21, 22). It was in *The Absorbent Mind* (1967a) that much information was recorded in great detail about Montessori's observations and ideas of how to care for the newborn. In modern Western hospitals most of what Montessori suggested for the newborn has been put into practice. Also, she explained to mothers how the first 3 years of life were the most important because the child had to learn more in these years than he would when he attended university.

Montessori was convinced that 'home life could be improved by training for motherhood' (Montessori, 1939: 12). Parents needed to be informed about the importance of the first 3 years of life along with the importance of understanding child development. Montessori talked repeatedly about the principles of Montessori education and child development and how parents could help development. She wrote newspaper articles, gave radio interviews and special lectures for parents. Importantly, she listened to parents. She helped parents to understand the creative work infants had to do from the moment of birth. Families could help by providing a peaceful environment, talking in quiet voices working about the child in an orderly way. She explained to parents that the mind was a spiritual embryo and every child had to construct his mind, construct his memory, absorb the language, learn to use every muscle and master his home environment. The child was helped by nature because he possessed an absorbent mind and an inner urge to move and learn. It was important for parents to understand how to help the child to develop and not hinder development because in the past 'adults have not understood the child or the adolescent' (Montessori, 1978: 11). Parents and children were the two poles of society.

Parents were assured by Montessori that they could help each child from birth by providing a calm, loving environment, ensuring the child was free of swaddling clothes and so able to exercise all muscles. Mother and child should remain close during the first days of life. Mothers could promote health by talking to the child and not placing the child in isolation. Montessori pointed out that a child who cried was more often lonely than hungry and an infant left in isolation could die of loneliness. The child's helper 'in early infancy has a noble task' (Montessori, 1967a: 103, 141, 135).

From the moment of birth the newborn is a social being. Parents had to understand that much had been observed by researchers of infant deaths in orphanages where it has been found that infants were often left alone for long periods of time.

Sensitive periods

Montessori mothers were helped to understand that from birth the child's mental life remained in a *sensitive period*. Physically the child was incomplete and Montessori noted 'the motor nerves are not yet provided with their covering of myelin . . . that enables them to transmit the brain's orders' (ibid.: 72). The child, she averred, must be free to move for motor nerves to develop to obey the brain. If a child was unable to move the connections between the brain and nerves, they remained incomplete and died. Mothers were to learn about the sensitive periods so they could learn how to help development.

Today, the concept of sensitive periods is no longer limited to Montessori education. Berk (1996: 27) defines a sensitive period as 'a time span that is optimal for certain capacities to emerge and in which the individual is especially responsive to the environmental influences'. She explains neurological evidence about the importance of the sensitive periods from birth when a baby 'is born with its full complement of neurones . . . and connecting nerve fibres grow at an astonishing rate. Connecting synapses frequently used, survived . . . those seldom used die off' (ibid.: 174). This corresponds with Montessori writings in 1939 about *myelization*. It helps to explain the importance of movement and repetition in child development from birth. Montessori encouraged parents to help development by providing the child with loose clothing to allow freedom of movement. A child has 'no behaviour foreordained at birth' as animals do. From the moment of birth the child 'is receiving impressions, he is an active seeker in his world' and needs favourable conditions from birth. Montessori noted that 'unfavourable conditions are so much worse, the wealthier the family into which he is born' because 'children are shut away in a nursery with no other companion than a nurse . . . who speaks to him seldom'. At birth the infant needs to be close to his mother and needs to hear conversations. The special relationship between mother and child begins at birth (Montessori, 1967a: 98, 100, 103). All development that follows depends on early care.

Montessori pointed out to parents that 'to recognise the great work of the child does not mean to diminish parents' authority' but she reminded them that 'parents are not the builders but the collaborators in the building process . . . their help becomes truly valuable . . . their authority comes from the help they are able to give their children . . . and their dignity rests solely on this' (Montessori, 1974: 16). Parents had to help the child from the earliest age to become independent from adults and learn to care for himself. At the same time Montessori expected parents to fight for the rights of children. Unconditional love of the child was the greatest aid in development (ibid.: 31). As the child lived in the family he became part of the family. Cohesive family life led to social cohesion when the child learned to put the family group first (Montessori, 1967a: 232). Montessori called for parents to change their ways of thinking about infants. She maintained that 'the baby knows best what he needs and lives in a world of his own interests' (Montessori Course, England, 1930). Montessori was asking parents to change their whole attitude towards child life from birth.

School/home relationships

When the child attended school, 'relationships between family, teacher and child should be harmonious'. Montessori made the pointed remark that parents with 'naughty children is due to a lack in the parents not the children . . . and if we are to make better conditions for the children we must consider parents' [sic] (Montessori Course, London, 1946). To Montessori, 'bad behaviour, naughtiness is an expression of deviant development, not normal development . . . and cannot be corrected by direct means'. The solution lay in providing the right environment and correct freedom which was 'an indirect treatment for curing naughtiness' (ibid.).

Although social life and family life may have changed since the first Casa dei Bambini in 1907, *child development has not changed.*

Montessori parents require education about how to compliment Montessori principles at home. They have to help their child from the earliest age to become independent. It is essential for parents to understand that it is too late to expect an adolescent to make good choices if he has never had the opportunity to make choices and think of the consequences from a young age. Similarly, it is unreasonable to expect a teenager to help with household chores and tidy his room if that has not been encouraged from 3 years. Parent evenings are held regularly in Montessori environments and parents are encouraged to share their varied cultural backgrounds. Worldwide, parents wish for the same thing – happy children who are healthy in body and mind.

Conclusions

Everything Maria Montessori introduced in 1907 was fresh and original. She abandoned traditional practices used in mainstream classrooms, particularly the teacher-centred approach which required children to sit motionless, listening mutely to the teacher talking, and learning through rote and memorization. The child experiencing such conditions she described as 'the forgotten citizen' in need of emancipation. Her huge contribution was to transfer education into a child-centred endeavour. Instead of rigidly directing everything within the classroom, the teacher followed and responded to each child's individual needs. Originally 'revolutionary', Montessori's philosophy and practice in 1907 included:

- understanding that children are unique individuals
- providing stress-free conditions in which children can learn
- equipping the room with Montessori didactic (self-teaching) materials
- giving children time to grasp a concept/skill at their own pace
- allowing children to feel unthreatened by competition
- encouraging children to work harmoniously with peers
- creating an environment offering children the thrill of learning more
- inculcating in children an enduring love of learning.

Child development

Above all else Montessori was a pioneer of child development. Everything done in the Casa dei Bambini in 1907 was related to child development. Her primary goal was the development of the whole child, a personality. Teachers and parents were obliged to understand the stages of development so they could help children's development.

Parents, she stressed, had the most important role during the first 3 years of life before their child entered the Casa. Parents and teachers collaborated in the education of children understanding that they could help development by providing stress-free conditions. As an anthropologist, Montessori observed children's natural tendencies and as a direct consequence, devised other unique features for her system. While observing social behaviour and development of 40 children in a multi-age environment, she realized young children were capable of learning more than she or others had imagined possible. Observation became the key tool of trade for Montessori directresses in understanding how to help children develop, and it became the principal instrument for assessing children's abilities, skills and knowledge. Montessori education was child-centred education based on the observations of free children.

Freedom and child development

Each child was to be recognized as a unique personality and treated as a distinctive human being. In the first Casa dei Bambini Montessori provided learning opportunities by introducing her didactic materials. Children's learning was never left to chance as the children were introduced to each piece of material individually by silent demonstration or a three-period lesson. She devised an environment where children were allowed to talk quietly, move about without constraint and socialize without disturbing those who were working. This stress-free environment was devoid of tests, exams, prizes, punishment or competition. The spectacular result was happy children. They unconsciously revealed their innate, natural tendencies which Montessori observed. These natural tendencies became the principles of Montessori education.

The individualized education gave children freedom to choose their own tasks according to their own interests, to work at their own rate for a long as they wished until their inner needs were satisfied, therefore Montessori saw little merit in a set agenda for all children.

The children were responsible for the curriculum they would follow by deciding what they would like to do. Materials were designed to attract children's attention. One of each piece of material was displayed on low shelf in easy reach of children. There were materials to help children learn to care for themselves, since Montessori maintained a child is not free unless he is independent (Montessori, 1964). By 6 years, a Montessori child (3–6 years) invariably showed indications of independence of mind, and on the way to becoming master of the environment and master of himself.

Children had rights, Montessori argued with passion, but they also had to learn that with freedom came responsibility to do the right thing along with awareness, to put the needs of the group before his own selfish needs. It was each child's right to be treated justly and receive the help he needed to become a successful learner.

In a Montessori environment every child at 4 years had the opportunity to learn to write and read using Montessori's original materials: metal insets, sandpaper letters and a movable alphabet.

Attention and information processing

Montessori observed children with deviant behaviour and noted that when they concentrated on a piece of didactic material which had attracted their attention, they became calm and contented, which she maintained was normal behaviour as nature intended. These children became *normalized*. They became self-disciplined, could work and live together in harmony and resolve differences themselves. Freedom led to self-discipline and both were seen by Montessori as interrelated.

It was 50 years later when Donald Broadbent (1958) produced one of the earliest models of information processing which he described as a theory of attention to explain what happened during listening tasks. It subsequently exerted an influence on the fields of cognitive psychology and cognitive development, and by the late 1970s, a consensus was emerging from the findings of behaviourists, learning theorists, cognitive psychologists, developmentalists and researchers of information processing. Information processing has been described as beginning in the learner's senses followed by application to a task. If the learner had the opportunity to practise and repeat an experience, the new information was learned and stored in Long Term Memory (LTM) (Gage and Berliner, 1979; Clarke-Stewart et al., 1985). After two decades of research, an interactive model of information processing had evolved which considered the interaction among the activities of the learner, the nature of the materials to be learned and the qualities of the task by which the learner was assessed (Brown et al., 1983). The interactive information processing model in 1983 was more closely matched to Montessori education than the stimulus/response model of behaviourist psychology put forth by researchers in 1907 when the first Casa dei Bambini opened. In a sense, all of these educators were catching up with the ideas Montessori had been propagating over half a century earlier about what goes on inside children's minds, how they learn and how they remember. Galloway pointed out:

> It is hard to understand how an instructional approach based on a philosophy that subsumes so many of the key ideas of the world's outstanding theorists of development, learning and education could have gone relatively unnoticed, particularly in the United States and Canada for a period of nearly fifty years.
>
> (Galloway, 1976: 412)

The relevance of Montessori education today

Montessori education is remarkably close to theories advanced by contemporary educators. Beyond dispute is the fact that it differs markedly from Pavlov's theory of conditioning, in vogue when she began her work. It is also worthy to note that during the last century many of Montessori's principles and materials have been integrated into mainstream early childhood education often without acknowledgement, while several important Montessori principles and practices from 1907 remain unique to Montessori education. The reader can decide which principles and practices remain unique to Montessori from the list below:

- children being treated with respect as unique individuals with individual needs
- children preparing themselves indirectly for the next stage of development by using didactic materials resulting in behaviour becoming normalized by six years
- observation of free children displaying mastery and understanding of the learning processes
- consideration for all children as they pass through developmental stages including the sensitive periods when children learn best leading them to write and read spontaneously at four years
- creation of a supportive stress-free environment with activities which engage children in higher order thinking
- children given help to construct knowledge through individual short three-period lessons
- children demonstrating success as they learn spontaneously through the use of Montessori didactic materials (including composing, spelling and reading)
- free children responsible for their own learning and empowered to choose their own areas and follow their own interests at their own pace, unthreatened by competition – no tests, no exams, no prizes, no punishments, no homework
- directresses who follow the psychic needs of each child at each stage of development with an eye to each child's development
- acknowledgement that each child has rights and responsibilities from the earliest age and that they are in the process of learning to become contributing members of their democratic classroom and later becoming contributing members of society
- recognition of social relationships, with active encouragement of social harmony during work and play, a positive fostering of social literacies through example, along with lessons in specific social graces and courtesies
- fundamental concern about the mental health of each child by providing therapeutic conditions for quality living in order to produce happy, normalized children.

Some unique practices in Montessori education have significant implications still to be considered for mainstream programmes today. Among these, of special note, is the high success rate of Montessori children learning to read and write spontaneously using Montessori didactic materials and methods. Mainstream education could, with profit, adopt this methodology.

Human qualities, seen by Montessori as being vital, are valued in Children's Houses today. Children are offered experiences in the following domains:

- Social – being truthful, cooperative, friendly, kind, confident
- Physical – refining small and large muscle control, moving with grace
- Intellectual – encouraging an interest in everything (Cosmic education)
- Aesthetic – loving beauty in nature, caring for the environment
- Emotional – through normalization, children become calm with nervous system at rest
- Spiritual – attitude from an inner urge, a love of life and being happy.

Such qualities become part of each child's character over the years in stress-free environments where they develop into cultured, refined, honourable, truthful, self-respecting adults. What stands out in Montessori schools is the behaviour of children, while not quantifiable, is observable in each child's actions and words.

Montessori successfully incorporated a number of elements in her individualized approach to education which:

- integrates children with special needs
- caters for the developmental needs of the whole child
- treats each child as an unique personality
- allows every child to meet success
- follows each child's psychic needs and interests
- meets the needs of modern society
- suits children of all ages, social backgrounds, cultures or race on every continent and in multicultural societies
- produces happy, mentally healthy, socially adjusted, contributing members of society
- is universal in these new times.

A well-balanced personality

Montessori children are encouraged to work with their hands and their minds, each normalized child possessing a well-balanced personality and equipped to relate harmoniously with others. It was Montessori's belief that if each child behaves in such a fashion daily in a stress-free environment at school and at home, it should be his routine behaviour when he takes his place in the wider community.

Mental health

Mental health remains a major issue for adolescents with calls today to find ways to curb youth suicide. Numbers of children suffering mental illnesses has risen to alarming figures with research showing that one in three suffers some mental health problem. Parents and teachers are advised to look for signs and seek help for children who are moody due to depression, using drugs, drinking alcohol, not sleeping, failing at school, suffering anxiety, being bullied physically or cyberbullying. Many turn to self-abuse with increasing numbers of children as young as 11 years committing suicide. Those in charge of education could benefit from a re-examination of Montessori's research. As early as 1909, Dr Crichton Miller reported 'that doctors of medicine and professors of psychology were saying her work would eventually make nerve specialists superfluous if the Montessori method was established in all schools' (Kramer, 1976: 264).

Montessori education is inclusive and integrates children with special needs. Much research has been done by Wendy Fidler who offers guidelines for Montessori teachers and parents caring for children with physical and mental disabilities. Her articles are found regularly in *Montessori International* (www.montessorimagazine.co) or by contacting wendyfidler@eight29.com.

Surveys and Interviews

(a few points from data collected in 2007)

It was found that Montessori directresses today:

- are particularly well informed about the special features of Montessori education
- are all noticeably committed in their efforts to following a whole – Montessori approach in practice
- provide for individual needs and treat children respectfully as individuals receiving respect in return
- understand the huge advantages of children becoming 'normalized' early
- endeavour to help children's mental health rather than allowing neurotic behaviour patterns continue
- do research in their own right and they treat each child as a case study
- share the common goal of helping develop happy, independent children.

One method for all children

Along with love, truth and respect, one method is used in Montessori education universally for all children from birth to adulthood: that is, provide for the psychic needs of each child at each stage of development. Montessori education is tailored for individual children from the earliest years preparing them to become independent learners and inevitably lifelong learners following their own interests. As they grow, children are helped to face reality by being better prepared to adapt and make responsible choices which are skills of special significance in our present age of rapid change.

Montessori education flourishes on every continent, and though still mainly part of the private system of education, it possesses qualities which could contribute much to the betterment of current practices within teacher education and mainstream education, especially literacy education. Contemporary studies in education appear to validate Montessori's theories and practices, much evidence being based on the observation of children.

Research findings

Research in the recent past, with its new interpretation of literacy learning (including socially-situated literacies and multiple literacies), appear to confirm the merits of Montessori practices. In Montessori environments special importance is laid on living in harmony and respecting the rights of others. In that regard, Montessori education fits happily into the thesis of Gee et al. (1996) who wrote about *Critical Social Literacy as a Millennium Literacy*. They argued that the literacies needed for the new millennium contain elements that have been practised and refined for thousands of years as well as new elements for this 'post everything age'. The new elements require finding ways of being humane on just and reciprocal bases and to be able to recognise and act on what is happening in society. Gee et al. claim that literacy is 'much more than being able to follow words across a page' (Mission and Christie, 1998). Further, they point out that 'intelligent people of any day or age aspire to lives of dignity and fulfilment for all and are prepared to collaborate in building it', but as these commentators warn, 'we need to be able to respond to distinctive conditions of lived in times' (ibid.: 175). Montessori seems to have anticipated these very conclusions at the beginning of the twentieth century.

Opportunities for further research

There are many opportunities for further inquiry in Montessori education. A few are listed here:

- Very little has been done to find the views of Montessori students, past and present, to ascertain:
  - the attitudes to the education they received including its strengths and weaknesses
  - the outcomes of their learning
  - the opinions of children withdrawn from a Montessori environment

- the opinions of children unable to adapt to the freedom given in a Montessori environment, unable to organize their own time and areas of study
- the attitudes of children with special needs
- the attitudes of children placed in a Montessori environment on the advice of psychologists.
- An investigation could be made to see how closely Montessori education matches the two new National Curricula proposed by governments in both the United Kingdom and in Australia.
- Research studies have not been done to compare Long Day Care Centres with Montessori Long Day Care centres for children from birth to school age children.
- What are the possibilities of introducing a Montessori component in all teacher training?
- How can Montessori education cater for all special needs children?
- How does working with Montessori materials affect the aged suffering the effects of dementia?

Montessori's vision of a new world in the future

In *Education and Peace* (1972), *Education for a New World* (1974) and other writings, Montessori spoke of her vision for a better world in which education would be the catalyst and principal agent for global harmony, peace and happiness. This new world would be realized not through adults but by way of children. There was a need for all humans to uplift themselves to the laws that govern (human) nature, she argued, and to reconnect to the laws of the universe which for millions of years had been a prerequisite for harmony among mankind (Lecture, late 1930s). Montessori envisaged a world where all people experienced social justice precisely as children in Montessori schools. She spoke of the 'universal child' growing into a young adult able to make wise choices in a free democratic world. Every graduate from school would be a cultured young adult fully prepared to adapt to an increasingly technological society no matter where he found himself as a world citizen. Her plan for new education for a new world involved helping the development of each child's unique personality from birth enabling him to become literate and equipping him to adapt and care for an unknown, fast changing technological world. Civilization, she felt, was at risk because while man had developed material things, he had in the process 'forgotten himself' (Lecture, India, 1946). The implication was that man's development had not kept up with material development, and little or no thought was given to the cosmic construction of one whole human society based on mutual help among men (ibid.). 'Humanity was on the down', she declared categorically, and all efforts in education needed to be directed towards raising humanity to a higher level (Lecture, Rome, 1951). That particular ideal of Montessori appears especially important today in a world where globalization and multiculturalism are realities. Montessori had considered relationships to be the crux of education and in today's unsettled global village it would appear that relationships among peoples of the world are increasingly vital for its very survival. As long as there are nations living with conflicts and turmoil in their everyday life there can be no world peace. She saw people as being world citizens and considered herself to be one.

At its heart, Montessori philosophy of education embraces mental health in general, especially peace of mind in each individual, peaceful homes and above all peaceful classrooms. Montessori saw all of these things as an indispensable preparation leading towards a peaceful world. Montessori education will be relevant and valuable in the future and merits closer attention by education practitioners and policymakers. The fundamental value of the Montessori Method lies in its origin, a thorough, clinical examination of the development of each unique child.

Bibliography

Adams, M. (1991), 'A talk with Marilyn Adams'. *Language Arts*, 68 (March), 206–12.

Anderson, M. (1929), 'The Montessori method'. *New Era*, 10.

Anderson, R. H. and Pavan, B. N. (1993), *Nongradedness: Helping It to Happen*. Lancaster, PA: Technomic.

Balson, M. (1992), 'Development of responsibility in students'. *Montessori Magazine* (Winter).

Beatty, H. M. (1922), *A Brief History of Education*. London: Watts.

Berk, L. E. (1996), *Infants, Children and Adolescents*. London: Allyn & Bacon.

Berryman, J. (1980), 'Montessori and Religious Education'. *Religious Education*, 75(3) (May–June), 294.

Beyer, E. (1962), 'Let's look at Montessori'. *Journal of Nursery Education*, 18(1) (November), 4–9.

Binet, A. and Simon H. (1905), 'Application des methods novelles au diagnostic noveau intellectual chez enfants normaux d'hospice et d'école primaire'. *L'Anne Psychologique*, 11, 245–66 and in Galloway, C. (1976), *Psychology for Learning and Teaching*. New York: McGraw-Hill.

Bingham, A. A., Dorta, P., McClasleay, M. and O'Keefe, J. (1995), *Exploring the Multiage Classrooms*. York, ME: Stenhouse.

Bissex, G. L. (1980), *Gnys at Work: A Child Learns to Write and Read*. Cambridge, MA: Harvard University Press.

Blenkin, G. M. and Kelly, A. V. (eds) (1996), *Early Childhood Education: A Developmental Curriculum*. London: Paul Chapman.

Bloget, R. (1979), *The Importance of the Development of the Senses*. California: Montessori World Educational Institute.

Boyd, Wm. (1917), *From Locke to Montessori. A Critical Account of the Montessori Point of View*. London: Harrap and Company.

— (1921), *The History of Western Education*. London: Adam Charles Black.

Bradley, L. and Bryant, P. E. (1983), 'Categorizing sounds and learning to read – a causal connection'. *Nature*, 301(5899), 419–21.

Broadbent, D. E. (1958), *Perception and Communication*. London: Pergamon.

Brown, A. L., Bransford, J. D., Ferrara, R. A. and Campione, J. C. (1983), 'Learning and understanding'. *Cognitive Development*, 3, 420–94 and in J. H. Flavell and E. M. Markman (eds), *Handbook of Child Psychology* (4th edn). New York: Wiley.

Bruner, J. S. (1960), *The Process of Education*. New York: Vintage Books.

— (1984), 'Vygotsky's zone of proximal development: The hidden agenda'. In B. Rogoff and J. V. Wertch (eds), *Children's Learning in the 'Zone of Proximal Development'*. San Francisco: Jossey-Bass. p. 23.

Burns, S., Griffin, P. and Snow, C. (eds) (1999), *Starting Out Right. A Guide to Promoting Children's Reading Success*. Washington, DC: National Research Council.

Butts, F. R. (1955), *A Cultural History of Western Education. Its Social and Intellectual Foundations*. New York: McGraw-Hill.

Byrne, B. and Fielding, B. R. (1991), 'Evaluation of a program to teach phonemic awareness to young children'. *Journal of Educational Psychology*, 83(4) (December), 451–5.

Cambourne, B. (1984), 'Language, learning and literacy. Another way of looking at language learning'. In A. Butler and J. Turbill (eds), *Towards a Reading Writing Classroom*. PETA, NSW: Roselle. Also in 1987 published in Portsmouth, New Hampshire: Heinemann.

Cambourne, B. and Rousch, P. (1980), 'There's more to reading than meets the eye'. *Australian Journal of Reading*, 3(2) (June), 107–14.

Carr, D. (1960), 'Art in Montessori schools'. *Communications* 2/3, 9–13. Amsterdam: Association Montessori Internationale.

Carr, W. and Kemmis S. (1986), *Becoming Critical: Education, Knowledge and Action Research*. Victoria, Australia: Deakin University Press.

Carroll, J. B. (1963), 'A model of learning'. *Teacher's College Record*, 64, 723–33.

Caspi, A. (1999), 'The child is the father of the man'. *Medical Research and Council News*, 80 (Winter/Spring).

Castells, M., Felda, R. and Freire P. (1999), *Critical Education in the New Information Age*. New York: Rowman & Littlefield.

Chattin-McNichols, J. (1991), 'Montessori teachers' intervention: Preliminary findings from an international study'. Paper presented at the Annual Conference of the National Association for the Education of Young Children. Denver, 7–10 November (ERIC ED 341 499).

— (1992), *The Montessori Controversy*. New York: Delmar.

Chomsky, C. (1971), 'Write first, read later'. *Childhood Education*, 47 (March), 196–9.

Christie, F. and Mission, R. (1998), *Literacy and Schooling*. London, UK: Routledge.

Clarke-Stewart, A., Friedman. S. and Koch, K. (1985), *Child Development: A Topical Approach*. New York : John Wiley & Sons.

Clay, M. M. I. (1998), *By Different Paths to Common Outcomes*. York, ME: Stenhouse.

Coe, E. J. (1991), 'Montessori education and its relevance to educational reform'. Paper presented at the Conference on the Future of Public Montessori Programs. New York, 17–19 October.

Cohen, S. (1974), 'The Montessori movement in England 1911–1952'. *History of Education*, 3(1).

Cole, L. (1950), *A History of Education: Socrates to Montessori*. New York: Rinehart.

Cole, M. (1999), 'PC classroom poses health risk for pupils'. *Courier Mail*. Education Report 3 (29 November).

Combs, A. W. (ed.) (1967), *Humanizing Education: The Person in the Process*. Washington, DC: Association for Supervision and Curriculum Development, National Education Association.

Corson, D. (1993), *Language, Minority Education and Gender. Linking Social Justice and Power*. Toronto, Canada: Ontario Institute for Studies in Education.

Courts, P. L. (1997), *Multicultural Literacies: Dialect, Discourse and Diversity*. Studies in Postmodern Theory of Education. New York: Peter Lang.

Crane, A. R. and Walker, W. G. (1957), *Peter Board: His Contribution to the Development of Education in New South Wales*. Melbourne: Australian Council for Education Research, pp. 196, 204, 299, 323.

Currie, J. and Breadmore, J. (1983), 'Montessori and Krishnamurti: A comparison of their educational philosophies and schools in practice in the USA and India'. In *Comparative and International Studies and the Theory and Practice of Education*. Proceedings of the Eleventh Annual Conference of the Australian Comparative and International Education Society. Hamilton, New Zealand, 21–24 August (ERIC ED 265 260 UD 024 660).

Cusack, G. (1997), 'Ukraine forms a Montessori Association and opens first teacher training center'. *Ukrainian Weekly*, 65(4) (26 January), 1–3.

Cushman, K. (1990), 'The whys and hows of the multi-age primary classroom'. *American Educator: The Professional Journal of the American Federation of Teachers*, 14(2) (Summer), 28–32, 39 (ERIC ED 412 628).

Dahl, K., Scharer, P. and Lawson, L. (1999), 'Phonics instruction and students achievement in whole language first grade classrooms'. *Reading Research Quarterly*, a journal of the International Reading Association, 34(3) (July/August/September), 312–41.

De Beer, Sir G. (1972), *Jean-Jacques Rousseau and His World*. London: Thames & Hudson.

D'Emidio-Caston, M. and Crocker, E. (1987), *Montessori Education: A Humanistic Approach for the 1990s*. Washington, DC: ERIC Clearing House.

Dewey, J. (1964), *John Dewey's Impressions of Soviet Russia and the Revolutionary World, Mexico-China-Turkey, 1929*. New York : Teachers College – Columbia University.

Donaldson, M. (1978). *Children's Minds*. Glasgow: Fontana/Collins.

Downing, J. and Oliver. P. (1973–4), 'The child's conception of a word'. *Reading Research Quarterly*, 9, 568–82.

Drummond, M. (1947), *Learning Arithmetic by the Montessori Method*. London: Harrup.

Duckworth, E. (1979), 'Either we are too early and they can't learn it or we're too late and they know it already: The dilemma of "Applying Piaget"'. *Harvard Educational Review*, 49(3), 297–312.

Duffy, M. 2001, Report on Attention Deficit Hyperactive Disorder, *Courier Mail* 6 April, p. 26.

Edelsky, C. (ed.) (1999), *Making Justice Our Project*. Teachers Working towards Critical Whole Language Practice. Illinois: National Council of teachers of English.

Edmonds, B. (1976), 'Comments on the Montessori philosophy and pre-school education in 1975'. *Developing Education*, 4(2) (August), 3–9.

Edmonson, B. (1963), 'Let's do more than look – let's research Montessori'. *Journal of Nursery Education*, 19 (November), 36–41.

Egan, K. (1983), *Education and Psychology: Plato, Piaget and Scientific Psychology*. London: Methuen.

Egan, K. and Nadaner, D. (1988), *Imagination and Education*. Milton Keyes: Open University Press.

Elkind, D. (1968), 'Piaget and Montessori'. *Education Digest*, 33 (March). Also reported in *Harvard Educational Review*, 37 (Fall), 535–45.

Epstein, P. (1990), 'Are public schools ready for Montessori?' *Principal*, 69(3) (May), 20–2 (ERIC ED 410 166).

Erikson, E. H. (1950), *Childhood and Society*. New York: W.W. Norton.

Evans, B. (1971), 'The absorbent mind'. *Leader*, 4(6), 61–3.

Fidler, W. (2004), Special needs children in Montessori environments. Dyslexia'; 'The Autistic Spectrum'; 'Dyspraxia'. A series of articles in *Montessori International*. Issues 69, 70, 71, 72.

Fields, M. V. and Spangler, L. (2000), *Let's Begin Reading Right* (4th edn). New Jersey: Merrill.

Fisher, D. C. (1913), *The Montessori Manual for Teachers and Parents*. Massachusetts: W.E. Richardson.

Frost, J. L. (1968), *Early Childhood Education Rediscovered* (Readings). New York: Holt, Rinehart & Winston.

Fynne, R. F. (1924), *Montessori and Her Inspirers*. New York: Longman.

Gage, N. L. and Berliner, D. C. (1979), *Educational Psychology*. Boston: Houghton Mifflin.

Gagné, R. (1965), *The Conditions of Learning*. London: Holt, Rinehart & Winston.

Galbraith, H. (1991), *Reasoning and Rhyming into Reading*. Ipswich Special Services Centre, Queensland: Department of Education.

Galloway, C. (1976), *Psychology for Learning and Teaching*. New York: McGraw-Hill.

Gardner, H. (1983), *Frames of Mind: The Theory of Multiple Intelligences*. New York: Basic Books.

Gee, J. P. (1996), *Social Linguistics and Literacies*. London: Taylor and Fracis.

Gee, J. P., Hull, G. and Lankshear, C. (1966), *The New Work Order: Behind the Language of the New Capitalism*. Sydney and Boulder, CO: Allen and Unwin.

Gillet, A. M. (1969), *Introduction to Biology*. Montessori Conference, Bergama, Italy. *Communications*, 4. Amsterdam: Association Montessori Internationale.

Good, H. G. (1983), *A History of Western Education*. London: Charles Black.

Goodman, K. (1994), 'Reading, writing and written texts: A transactional sociopsycholinguistic view'. In R. Ruddell, M. Ruddell and H. Singer (eds), *Theoretical Models and Processes of Reading* (4th edn). Newark, DE: International Reading Association in USA.

Goodman, Y. M. (1987), 'Kid watching: An alternative to testing'. *National Elementary Principal*, 57(4) (June), 41–5.

Graves, D. (1982), 'Patterns of child control of the writing process'. In *Donald Graves in Australia. 'Children want to write . . .'*. Rozelle: PETA, 17–28.

Grazzini, C. (1975), 'The International Centre for Montessori Studies Foundation'. *Communications*, 2. Amsterdam: Association Montessori Internationale.

Guthrie, E. R. (1952), *The Psychology of Learning*. New York: Harper.

Hainstock, E. G. (1971), *Teaching Montessori in the Home: The School Years*. New York: Plume Book/New American Library.

Haliday, M. A. K. (1975), *Learning How to Mean: Explorations in the Development of Language (Explorations in Language Study)*. London: Edward Arnold.

Hall, N. (1987), *The Emergence of Literacy*. London: Hodder & Stroughton.

Hans, N. (1994), *Comparative Education: A Study of Educational Factors and Traditions*. London: Routledge & Kegan Paul.

Hart, M. (2001), 'Kids on the edge'. Report from the national survey of Mental Health and Wellbeing, Canberra, *Courier Mail*, 14 March.

Henderson, E. H. (1984), 'Understanding Children's knowledge of written Language'. In D. B. Yaden and S. Templeton (1988), *Metalinguistic Awareness and Beginning Literacy*. Portsmouth: H.H. Heinemann.

Holdaway, D. (1979), *The Foundations of Literacy*. New York: Ashton Scholastic.

Holman, H. (1925), *Séguin and His Philosophical Method of Education*. London: Adam Black.

Holt, J. (1974), *How Children Fail*. Manchester: Penguin Books.

Hunt, J. McV. (1961), 'Intelligence and experience'. In Introduction to Montessori, M. (1964) *The Montessori Method*. New York: Ronald, pp. xi–xxxv.

— (1964), *The Montessori Method*, New York: Schocken Books.

— (1974), 'How children develop intellectually'. *Children*, 11(3), 83–92.

Itard, J. M. G. (1801), *Des Primiers Development du Jeune Savage de l'Averyon*. Translated as *The Wild Boy of Averyon*, by G. and M. Humphrey (1932). New York: Appleton-Century.

James, Wm. (1890), *The Principles of Psychology*. New York: Holt.

Joosten, A. M. (1995), *The Montessori Movement in India*. Madras: India Montessori Training Courses.

— (1969), 'Gandhi and Maria Montessori'. *Communications*, 2(3), 21–3. Amsterdam: Association Montessori International.

— (1973), Preface in Maria Montessori, *From Childhood to Adolescence*. New York: Schocken Books. First published in 1948.

Kahn, D. (ed.) (1995). *What Is Montessori Preschool?* North American Teachers Association in affiliation with Association Montessori Internationale, Amsterdam.

— (2005), 'Montessori Erdkinder: The social evolution of the Little Community'. Paper presented at the Twenty-Fifth International Montessori Congress. Sydney.

Kaplan, P. S. (1991), *A Child's Odyssey.* New York: West.

Kilpatrick, W. H. (1914), *The Montessori System Examined.* Boston: Houghton Miffin.

Kneller, G. F. (1951), 'Education in Italy'. In A. H. Moehlman and J. S. Roucek (eds), *Comparative Education.* New York: Holt, Rhinehart & Winston.

Kohlberg, L. (1964), 'Development of moral character and moral ideology'. In L. W. Hoffman and M. L. Hoffman (eds), *Review of Child Development Research*, vol. 1. New York: Russell Sage Foundation.

Kohn, A. (1993), *Punished by Awards.* New York: Houghton-Miffin.

Kong, S. L. (1970), *Humanistic Psychology and Humanized Teaching.* Toronto: Holt, Rinehart & Winston.

Kramer, R. (1976), *Maria Montessori: A Biography.* Oxford: Basil Blackwell.

Krogh, S. L. (1984), 'Preschool democracy – Ideas from Montessori'. *Social Studies*, 75(4) (June/August), 176–81 (ERIC ED 303 480).

Lankshear, C., Gee, J., Knoble, M. and Searle, C. (1997), *Changing Literacies.* Philadelphia: Open University Press.

Lawson, J. and Silver, H. (1973), *A Social History of Education in England.* London: Methuen.

Lawson, M. D. (1974), 'Montessori: The Indian years'. *Forum of Education*, 33(1), 36–49.

Lillard, P. P. (1972), *Montessori. A Modern Approach.* New York: Schocken Books.

Loeffler, M. (ed.) (1992), *Montessori in Contemporary American Culture.* Portsmouth, NH: Heinemann.

Lohmann, R. T. (1988), 'A re-vision of Montessori: Connections with Dewey, Piaget and Vygotsky'. US Department of Educational Resources Information Center (ERIC ED 304 210).

Luke, A. and Gilbert, P. (1993) *Literacy in Context – Australian Perspectives and Issues.* Singapore: Allen & Unwin.

Lundberg, I. (1988), Are Letters Necessary in the Development of Phonological Awareness? A paper presented at the Twelfth World Congress on Reading, International Reading Association, Australia, July.

Maccheroni, A. M. (1947), *A True Romance: Dr Maria Montessori as I Knew Her.* Edinburgh: Oliver & Boyd.

McAllister, A. (1999), *Strathclyde People.* Glasgow, Scotland: University of Strathclyde Magazine.

McClay, J. L. (1996), *The Multiage Classroom.* Sydney: Hawker Brownlow Education.

MacDonald, B. and Walker, R. (1976), *Changing the Curriculum.* Bath: Pitman.

Mallett, M. (1999), *Young Researchers: Informational Reading and Writing in the Earl and Primary Years*. London: Routledge.

Martin, N. (1976), *Interaction in the Classroom. London*: Methuen.

Martin, R. D. (1991), 'Empowering teachers to break the basal habit'. Paper presented at the Thrity-Sixth Annual Meeting of the International Reading Association. Las Vegas, NV, 6–10 May.

Martin, Y. (1999), *Avshalom Caspi, The Child is Father of the Man* Medical Research Council News, Winter/Spring, no. 80.

Merrill, J. B. (1909), 'New method in kindergarten education'. *Kindergarten Primary Magazine*, 32(4), 106–7, 142–4, 211–21, 297–8.

Militich-Conway, B. and Openshaw, R. (1988), 'The Montessori method in Wanganui education board district 1911–1924'. *New Zealand Journal of Educational Studies*, 23(2), 189–200.

Miller, G. A. (1956), 'The magical number seven, plus-or-minus two. Some limits on our capacity for processing information'. *Psychological Review*, 63(2), 81–97.

Montanaro, S. Q. (1990), *The Importance of the First Three Years of Life*. Mountain View, CA: Nienhuis.

Montessori, M. (1910), *Pedagogical Anthropology*. Publishing details unknown.

— (1928), *The Child in the Church*. Catholic liturgy from child's point of view. London: Sands. First published in 1922 in Naples.

— (1956), *The Child in the Family*. London: Chaucer.

— (1961 [1948]), *What You Should Know about Your Child*. Madras, India: Kalakshetra.

— (1964 [1909]), *The Montessori Method*. New York: Schocken Books.

— (1965a [1941]), *The Child*. Adyar, Madras, 20: Vasanta, The Theosophical Society.

— (1965b [1914]), *Dr Montessori's Own Handbook*. NewYork: Schocken Books.

— (1965c [1916]), *Spontaneous Activity in Education. The Advanced Montessori Method*, vol. 1. New York: Schocken Books.

— (1967a [1939]), *The Absorbent Mind*. New York: Dell.

— (1967b [1929]), *The Discovery of the Child*. Madras, India: Kalakshetra.

— (1971 [1942]), *Reconstruction in Education*. Madras, India: Theosophical Publishing House.

— (1972 [1932]), *Education and Peace*. Chicago: Regnery.

— (1973a), *From Childhood to Adolescence*. New York: Schocken Books.

— (1973b [1916]), *The Montessori Elementary Material. The Advanced Montessori Method*, vol. 2. New York: Schocken Books.

— (1973c [1946]), *To Educate the Human Potential*. Madras, India: Kalakshetra.

— (1974 [1946]), *Education for a New World*. Madras, India: Kalakshetra.

— (1975 [1948]), *The Formation of Man*. Madras, India: Kalakshetra.

— (1978 [1936]), *The Secret of Childhood*. Hyderabad, India: Orient Longman.

— (1980), *Childhood Education*. New York: Meridian.

— (1996), *The Child, Society and the World: Unpublished Speeches and Writings*. The Clio Montessori Series. Oxford, UK: Clio.

— (1997), *Ideas of Montessori's Educational Theory*. Extracts from Maria Montessori's writings and teachings. The Clio Montessori Series, vol. 14. Compiled by Paul Oswald and Günter Schultz-Benesch. Translated from German by Lawrence Salmon. Oxford, UK: Clio.

Montessori, M. (1972), 'Voices from the past . . . and present'. *Communications*, 6, 2–6. Amsterdam: Association Montessori Internationale.

Montessori, M. Jr (1976), *Education for Human Development: Understanding Montessori*. New York: Schocken Books.

Montessori, R. (2005), *Educateurs sans Frontières*. Amsterdam: Nienhuis.

Müller, T. and Schneider, R. (eds) (2002), *Montessori Teaching Materials 1913–1935. Furniture and Architecture*. Berlin: Prestel.

Muspratt, S., Luke, A. and Freebody, P. (eds) (1997), *Constructing Critical Literacies. Teaching-Learning Textual Practice*. New South Wales: Allen & Urwin.

Mussen, P. H. (ed) (1917), *Manual of Child Psychology*. New York: Wiley.

Nasgaard, S. (1929), 'The Montessori movement in Denmark'. *The New Era*, 10, 61–6.

Neill, A. S. (1962), *Summerhill*. Hammondsworth: Penguin.

Nunn, Sir P. (1920), *Education: Its Data and First Principles*. London: Edward Arnold.

O'Donnell, D. (1996), *Montessori Education in Australia and New Zealand*. NSW: Fast Books.

Olaf, M. (2008), *Child of the World*. Arcata, CA.

Orem, R. C. (1967), *Montessori for the Disadvantaged*. New York: G.P. Pitman's Sons.

Ornstein, A. C. (1977), *An Introduction to the Foundations of Education*. London: Rand McNally Education Series.

Owen, R. (1997), *The Story of Robert Owen (1771–1858)*. New Lanark, Scotland: Conservation Trust.

Petersen, R. C. (1968), 'The Montessorians – M.M. Simpson and Lillian de Lissa'. In C. Turney (ed.) (1972), *Pioneers of Australian Education*. Sydney: Sydney University Press. 240–8.

— (1971), 'Montessori *in* Australia'. *Education News*, 13.

Phillips, S. (1979), 'Maria Montessori and contemporary cognitive psychology'. *British Journal of Teacher Education*, 3(1) (January), 55–8.

— (1980), 'New fashions in child rearing and education'. *New Horizons in Education*, 62 (Autumn).

Piaget, J. (1974), *To Understand Is to Invent*. New York: Viking.

Piers, M. W. (1978), *Infanticide*. New York: W.W. Norton.

Potts, A. (1980), 'Montessori – A progressive educator?' *The Forum of Education. An Australian Journal of Education*, 39(3) (September), 26–34.

Prakasam, G. A. (1948), Foreword of Montessori's *What You Should Know about Your Child*. Law Library, Colombo, Madras: Kalakshetra.

Rambusch, N. (1962), *Learning How to Learn.* Baltimore: Helican.

Raymont, T. (1937), *A History of the Education of Young Children.* London: Longman's Green Co.

Read, C. (1975), *Children's Categorization of Speech Sounds in English.* Urbanana: National Council of Teachers of English.

Renwick, A. (1967), 'A modern impression of the Montessori method', *Australian Journal of Education*, 11.

Riordan, C. (1997), *Equality and Achievement*: *An Introduction to the Sociology of Education.* New York: Longman.

— (1961) Round the child Association of Montessorians, Vol. 6, p. 6, Calcutta.

Schill, B. and E. Omwake (1963), 'The Montessori System'. *Childhood Education* (December), Association for Childhood Education International, 39, 171–6.

Schill, B. (1974). *The Montessori System. Childhood Education,* December. Association for Childhood Education International.

Schiller, P. (2000), 'Key findings in brain research development: Brain research applications'. One day Workshop, Creche and Kindergarten Association. Newmarket, Brisbane, 14 June.

Schneir, W. and Schneir, M. (1971), 'The joy of learning – in the open corridor'. *New York Magazine* (4 April), 30–1, 72–97.

Schonell, F. J. (1945), *The Psychology and Teaching of Reading* (3rd edn). Edinburgh: Oliver & Boyd.

Schonell, F. J. and Cochrane, R. G. (1962), *The Slow Learner: Segregation or Integration.* St Lucia: University of Queensland press.

Schulz-Benesch, G. (1997), *Basic ideas of Montessori's Educational Theory.* Extracts from Maria Montessori's writings and teachings. The Clio Montessori Series, Vol. 14. Translated from the German by Lawrence Salmon. Oxford: Clio Press.

Séguin, E. (1866a), *Idiocy: And Its Treatment by the Physiological Method.* Albany: Columbia University Teachers College Educational Reprints, 1907.

— (1866b), *Traitment Moral, Hygiène des Idiots.* Paris: Bibliotheque d'education speciale, 1906.

Seldin, T. and Epstein, P. (2003), *The Montessori Way – An Education for Life.* Florida: Montessori Foundation.

Shore, M. (1995), 'Students as tutors in early childhood settings: The acquisition and transmission of problem solving skills'. Paper presentation at BP International Conference. London, England.

Silberman, C. E. (ed.) (1973), *The Open Classroom Reader.* New York: Vintage Books.

Simons, J. L. and Simons, F. A. (1984), 'Montessori and regular preschools: A comparison, ERIC, Clearing House of Elementary and Early Childhood Education, Urbana, Illinois'. To be published in Katz, L. G. (ed.), *Current Topics in Early Childhood Education.* Norwood, NJ: Ablex Publishing Corporation (ERIC ED 247 031).

Simpson, M. M. (1914), *Report on the Montessori Methods of Education*. Sydney: Government Printer.

Smith, T. (1912), *The Montessori System*. New York and London: Harper Brothers.

Springer, J. (1991), *Listen to Us: The World of Working Children*. Sydney: Allen & Unwin.

Standing, E. M. (1957), *Maria Montessori: Her Life and Her Work*. London: Hollis & Carter.

— (1966), *The Montessori Revolution in Education*. New York: Schocken Books.

Stenhouse, L. (1975), *An Introduction to Curriculum Research and Development*. London: Heinemann.

Strathclyde People Magazine (1999), Glasgow, Scotland: University of Strathclyde.

Straker, L. (1999) in Cole, M. Cassroom poses health risk for pupils, Courier Mail. Educational Report, 29 November, p. 3.

Street, B. (1995), *Social Literacies: Critical Approaches to Literacy in Development, Ethnography and Education*. London: Longman.

Stubbs, B. (1966), 'Montessori and her influence on our work today'. *Australian Pre-school Quarterly*, (6 May).

Sullivan, H. G. (1985), 'Maria Montessori: Pioneer of an unique method of education', *The Australian Women's Weekly* (March), 252–3.

Thorn, M. E. (1951), 'Dr Montessori in the home'. Paper presented at International Montessori Congress, London. Montessori Trust (Scotland), Edinburgh: Darien.

Thorndike, E. L. (1906), *Principles of Teaching Based on Psychology*. New York: Seiler.

Tunmer, W. E., Pratt, C. and Herriman, M. L. (1984), *Metalinguistic Awareness in Children. Theory, Research and Implications*. Canada: Springer-Verlag.

Turney, C. (1972), *Pioneers of Australian Education* (2nd edn). Sydney: Sydney University Press.

Vygotsky, L. S. (1934), *Thought and Language*. Published (1986), Cambridge, MA: MIT.

— (1978), *Mind in Society: The Development of Higher Psychological Processes*. Cambridge, MA: Harvard University.

Watson, J. B. (1914), *Behaviour, An Introduction to Comparative Psychology*. New York: Holt.

Weber, L. (1971), *The English Infant School – Informal Education*. Englewood Cliffs, NJ: Prentice-Hall.

Wertsch, J. V. (ed.) (1985), *Vygotsky and the Social Formation of the Mind*. Cambridge, MA: Harvard University Press.

Wider, E. L. (1970), *The Critical Years: Early Childhood Education at the Crossroads*. Pennsylvania: International Textbook.

Willcott, P. (1968), 'The initial American reception of the Montessori method'. *Education Digest*, 34 (October), condensed from *School Review*, 76 (June), 147–65, University of Amman.

Wolf, A. (1996), *Nurturing the Spirit in Non-Sectarian Classrooms*. Hillidaysburg, PA: Parent Child.

Wood, M. (1994), *Essentials of Classroom Teaching: Elementary Language Arts.* Needham Heights, MA: Allyn & Bacon.

Wretch, J. V. (1984), 'Zone of proximate development: Some conceptual issues', in B. Rogoff and J. B. Wretch (eds), *Children's Learning in the Zone of Proximal Development. New Directions for Child Development.* San Francisco, CA: Jossey-Bass.

Yopp, H. and Singer, H. (1994), 'Toward an interactive reading instruction model: Explanation of activation of linguistic awareness and metalinguistics ability in learning to read'. In R. Ruddell, M. Ruddell and H. Singer (eds), *Theoretical Models and Processes of Reading,* 4th edn. Newark: DE: International Reading Association.

Yussen, S. R. (1980), 'Performance of Montessori and traditionally schooled nursery children on social cognitive tasks and memory problems'. *Contemporary Educational Psychology,* 5(2) (April), 124–37.

Definitions of Some Montessori Terms

Absorbent mind | The unconscious way in which a young child from birth to about 6 years learns easily from his environment.

Casa dei Bambini | Italian for 'Children's House'.

Cosmic education | Each child is helped to develop his whole personality by being introduced to a wide curriculum.

Deviant child | A child who experiences difficulty concentrating on any 'thing'. He lacks self-control and sometimes escapes into a world of fantasy.

Didactic materials | Self-teaching materials which make self-correction possible.

Directress | Montessori's name for a 'new' type of teacher.

Formative years | The important years between birth and 6 years when a child creates his character from the environment with the help of his absorbent mind.

Horme | A vital inner urge (inner voice) by which a child is able to choose activities which best suit his development at a particular time.

Liberty | Freedom to be active within an educational framework of structure and discipline where each child has rights. Liberty includes freedom of the mind.

Mental health	Good mental health brings peace of mind.
Muscular memory	A child's ability to remember the name of something when he moves his fingers over the object. For example, when a child traces a sandpaper letter he has already been introduced to, he can recall the sound the letter represents immediately through his muscular memory.
Normalized	A child who is calm, happy, self-controlled, adapts easily, and who develops into a well-balanced adolescent and adult.
Order	The meaning given to everything within a child's environment which in turn helps him to organize his own mind and to classify what he finds within the environment.
Phonetic words	Phonetically regular words are introduced to English-speaking children in order of length – first, three-letter phonetic words followed by longer phonetic words for composing and before using beginning phonetic reading books.
Phonograms	These appear in non-phonetic words and are made up of two or more letters which combine to make one sound; for example, ay, ea, igh, ough.
Prepared environment	Peaceful and orderly surroundings adapted to children's interests, including the living conditions which enable the child to have the freedom to choose and concentrate on his own tasks, to learn through his own activity, and provides the basis for development of each child's personality.

Psychic embryo	The inborn order through which the child's mental functions are developed over a long period of time.
Sensitive periods	Developmental periods when a child is particularly sensitive to learning specific things. For example, to begin to take a few steps at 10 months, to speak single words about the same time, to begin to write and read at 4 years.
Sensorial exercises	Exercises using didactic materials designed to help development and refine all the senses, providing a foundation for all later learning.
Spirit	The life of the mind.
The three-period lesson	The three-period lesson is brief, simple and objective. The directress uses few words so the child can focus on the object of the lesson.

Index